# The Healing Power of Foods Cookbook

## Over 150 Delicious Meat-Free Recipes for Vibrant Health

◆ ◆ ◆ ◆

### Michael T. Murray, N.D.

**Prima Publishing**
P.O. Box 1260BK
Rocklin, CA 95677
(916) 786-0426

Production by Melanie Field, Bookman Productions
Composition by WESType
Interior design by Suzanne Montazer
Cover design by The Dunlavey Studio, Sacramento
Cover photo by Kent Lacin

**Library of Congress Cataloging-in-Publication Data**

Murray, Michael T.
    The healing power of foods cookbook : over 150 delicious meat-free recipes for vibrant health / Michael T. Murray.
      p.   cm.
    Includes index.
    ISBN 1-55958-318-5 (pbk.) :
    1. Vegetarian cookery.  2. Nutrition.  I. Title.
TX837.M868    1993
641.5'636—dc20                    93-3298
                                           CIP

97 98 99 00  AA  10 9 8 7 6 5 4 3 2

Printed in the United States of America

**How to Order:**

Quantity discounts are available from the publisher, Prima Publishing, P.O. Box 1260BK, Rocklin, CA 95677; telephone: (916) 786-0426. On your letterhead include information concerning the intended use of the books and the number of the books you wish to purchase.

# · · · · ·Contents

# ·····*Acknowledgments*

I would like to thank the staff nutritionists (Brenda, Barbara, Kristin, and Daniella) at Trillium Health Products for their help in putting this cookbook together. I would also like to thank everyone at Prima Publishing and Bookman Productions, especially Ben, Jennifer, Melanie, and Steve, for their efforts.

# ••••*Eating for Health*

Have you ever heard the expression "You are what you eat"? Have you ever thought about what determines the composition of your body? Although genetics certainly plays a role, the foods you eat provide the materials that make up who you are. Thus, you certainly are what you eat. And whether you are in a state of poor health or simply desire better health, improving the quality of the foods you regularly consume is a must.

The human body is the most remarkable machine in the world, but most Americans are not feeding their body the high-quality fuel it deserves. When a machine does not receive the proper fuel or maintenance, how long will it run efficiently? If your body is not fed the full range of nutrients it needs, how can you expect it to remain in a state of good health?

Appreciation of the role of diet in determining our level of health is growing rapidly. It is now well established that certain dietary practices cause—and others prevent—a wide range of diseases. In addition, more and more research indicates that certain diets and foods offer immediate therapeutic benefits.

The *Healing Power of Foods Cookbook* is packed with delicious recipes that use wholesome, natural foods. This cookbook is designed to be used in conjunction with *The Healing Power of Foods* to inspire you to make more healthful food choices. Together these books will teach you about the foods your body needs to maintain or return to health.

The recipes contained in this cookbook focus on plant-based foods—vegetables, fruits, grains, legumes, nuts, and seeds. The human body appears to be better suited to a diet composed primarily of these foods—a contention supported not only by detailed evaluations of human anatomy and physiology, but by voluminous evidence showing that deviation from a predominantly plant-based diet is a major factor in the development of heart disease, cancer, strokes, arthritis, and many other chronic degenerative diseases. Because these diseases have reached epidemic proportions in the United States, many health and medical organizations now recommend that the human diet should focus primarily on plant-based foods.

In an attempt to create a new model in nutrition education, the USDA developed the "Eating Right Pyramid" (see Figure 1.1). The pyramid does not change the USDA's previous list of essential food groups per se; instead, it visually stresses the importance of making fresh fruits, vegetables, and whole grains the basis of a healthy diet. Many medical experts, however, feel the USDA Eating Right Food Pyramid simply does not make a strong enough statement. The Physicians' Committee for Responsible Medicine, a nonprofit organization based in Washington, D.C., has proposed that the New Four Food Groups of Fruits, Vegetables, Grains, and Legumes be used as an alternative to the Eating Right Food Pyramid. Foods obviously missing from this proposed model are meat and dairy products. The Physicians' Committee proposed that these foods be considered optional under the new plan. From a health-promotion standpoint, the New Four Food Groups system offers the best guidelines.

Vegetables, fruits, grains, and legumes (beans) form the foundation of a healthful diet. However, most Americans do not consume enough of these foods. One reason may be a lack of familiarity with recipes that use these foods. Cooking and

**Figure 1.1**  The Eating Right Pyramid of Foods

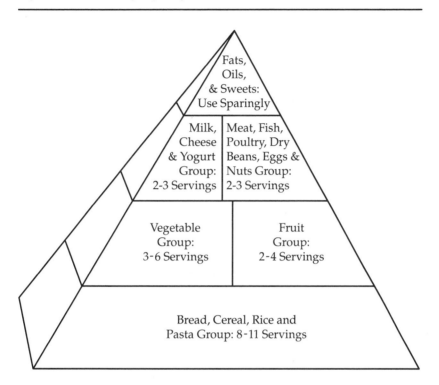

eating for health is not a difficult process. It may take a little forethought, but the payoff is well worth it.

This cookbook is full of deliciously nutritious recipes that rely on health-promoting foods. Each recipe is clearly described and includes a detailed nutritional analysis and the number of servings it provides according to the Healthy Exchange Lists.

## The Healthy Exchange System

The American Dietetic Association and the American Diabetes Association, in conjunction with other groups, have developed a convenient tool—the ADA exchange system—for rapidly estimating the calorie, protein, fat, and carbohydrate content of a diet. Originally intended to be used in designing dietary recommendations for diabetics, the exchange method is now used in calculating and designing virtually all therapeutic diets. Unfortunately, the ADA exchange plan does not focus sharply enough on the quality of food choices. The Healthy Exchange System, presented in full in *The Healing Power of Foods* and in an abbreviated form here, is a more healthful version because it emphasizes better food choices and unprocessed, whole foods.

The diet is prescribed by allotting the number of exchanges allowed per list for one day. There are seven exchange lists, although the milk and meat lists should be considered optional:

*The Healthy Exchange System*
    List 1–Vegetables
    List 2–Fruits
    List 3–Breads, Cereals, and Starchy Vegetables
    List 4–Legumes
    List 5–Fats
    List 6–Milk
    List 7–Meats, Fish, Cheese, and Eggs

All food portions within each exchange list provide approximately the same amounts of calories, proteins, fats, and carbohydrates per serving. Table 1.1 lists macro-nutrient composition per serving.

## The Healthy Exhange Lists

### List 1–Vegetables

Vegetables are excellent sources of vitamins, minerals, and health-promoting fiber compounds. Vegetables are fantastic "diet" foods, since they are very high in nutritional value but low in calories. Starchy vegetables such as potatoes and

**Table 1.1** Macro-Nutrient Composition per Serving

| List | Protein (g) | Fat (g) | Cholesterol (g) | Fiber (g) | Calories (kcal) |
|---|---|---|---|---|---|
| Vegetables | 3 | 0 | 11 | 1–3 | 50 |
| Fruits | 0 | 0 | 20 | 1–3 | 80 |
| Breads, etc. | 2 | 0 | 15 | 1–4 | 70 |
| Legumes | 7 | 0.5 | 15 | 6–7 | 90 |
| Fats | 0 | 5 | 0 | 0 | 45 |
| Milk | 8 | 0 | 12 | 0 | 80 |
| Meats, etc. | 7 | 3 | 0 | 0 | 55 |

yams are included in List 3 (Breads, Cereals, and Starchy Vegetables). In addition to being eaten whole, vegetables can be consumed as fresh juice. There is also a list of "free" vegetables, which can be eaten in any desired amount. These vegetables are termed "free foods" because the calories they supply are offset by the number of calories your body burns in the process of digesting them. These foods are especially valuable as diet foods because they help keep you feeling satisfied between meals.

Because the recommended consumption level for vegetables under the Healthy Exchange System is quite high, many people find it helpful to juice their fresh, raw vegetables. Juicing allows for easy absorption of the health-giving properties of fresh fruits and vegetables in larger amounts.

Each of the following equals one vegetable exchange:

1 cup cooked vegetables

2 cups raw vegetables

1 cup fresh vegetable juice

### List 2–Fruits

Fruits make excellent snacks because they contain fructose (fruit sugar). This sugar is absorbed relatively slowly into the bloodstream, thereby allowing the body time to utilize it. Fruits are also excellent sources of vitamins, minerals, and health-promoting fiber compounds. However, fruits are less nutrient-dense than vegetables, because they are typically higher in calories. That is why vegetables are favored over fruits in weight-loss plans and overall healthful diets.

Each of the following quantities equals one fruit exchange:

1 cup fresh or cooked unsweetened fruit

1/2 cup cooked sweetened fruit

1 cup fresh juice

2/3 cup pasteurized fruit juice

1 tablespoon honey, sugar, jam, jelly, or preserves

## List 3–Breads, Cereals, and Starchy Vegetables

Breads, cereals, and starchy vegetables are classified as complex carbohydrates. Chemically, complex carbohydrates are made up of long chains of simple carbohydrates or sugars. The body has to digest or break down the large sugar chains into simple sugars before it can make use of these sugars. Therefore, the sugar from complex carbohydrates enters the bloodstream at a slower rate, allowing blood-sugar levels and appetite to be better controlled.

Complex carbohydrate foods such as breads, cereals, and starchy vegetables are higher in fiber and nutrients but lower in calories than are foods with a high simple-sugar content, such as cakes and candies.

Each of the following quantities equals one bread exchange:

*Breads*

| | |
|---|---|
| Bagel, small | 1/2 |
| Dinner roll | 1 |
| Dried bread crumbs | 3 tablespoons |
| English muffin, small | 1/2 |

| | |
|---|---|
| Tortilla (6-inch) | 1 |
| Whole wheat, rye, or pumpernickel | 1 slice |

*Cereals*

| | |
|---|---|
| Bran flakes | 1/2 cup |
| Cornmeal (dry) | 2 tablespoons |
| Cereal (cooked) | 1/2 cup |
| Flour | 2 1/2 tablespoons |
| Grits (cooked) | 1/2 cup |
| Pasta (cooked) | 1/2 cup |
| Puffed cereal (unsweetened) | 1 cup |
| Rice or barley (cooked) | 1/2 cup |
| Wheat germ | 1/4 cup |
| Other unsweetened cereal | 3/4 cup |

*Crackers*

| | |
|---|---|
| Arrowroot | 3 |
| Graham (2 1/2-inch square) | 2 |
| Matzo (4-inch × 6-inch) | 1/2 |
| Rye wafers (2-inch × 3 1/2-inch) | 3 |
| Saltines | 6 |

*Starchy vegetables*

| | |
|---|---|
| Corn | 1/3 cup |
| Corn on cob | 1 small |
| Parsnips | 2/3 cup |
| Potato, mashed | 1/2 cup |
| Potato, white | 1 small |
| Squash, winter, acorn, or butternut | 1/2 cup |

| | |
|---|---|
| Yam or sweet potato | 1/4 cup |

*Prepared foods*

| | |
|---|---|
| Biscuit, 2-inch diameter (omit 1 fat exchange) | 1 |
| Corn bread, 2-inch × 2-inch × 1-inch (omit 1 fat exchange) | 1 |
| French fries, 2 to 3 inches long (omit 1 fat exchange) | 8 |
| Muffin, small (omit 1 fat exchange) | 1 |
| Pancake, 5-inch × 1/2-inch (omit 1 fat exchange) | 1 |
| Potato or corn chips (omit 2 fat exchanges) | 15 |
| Waffle, 5-inch × 1/2-inch (omit 1 fat exchange) | 1 |

### List 4–Legumes

Legumes (beans) are rich in important nutrients and health-promoting compounds. Legumes help improve liver function, lower cholesterol levels, and improve blood-sugar control. Since obesity and diabetes has been linked to the loss of blood-sugar control (insulin insensitivity), legumes appear to be extremely important in weight-loss plans and in the dietary management of diabetes.

For any type of cooked or sprouted beans, 1/2 cup equals one legume exchange.

## List 5–Fats and Oils

Animal fats, which are typically solid at room temperature, are referred to as saturated fats; while virtually all vegetable fats are liquid at room temperature and are referred to as unsaturated fats or oils. Vegetable oils provide excellent sources of the essential fatty acids linoleic acid and linolenic acid. These fatty acids function in our bodies as components of nerve cells, cellular membranes, and hormonelike substances. Fats also provide the body with energy.

While fats are important to human health, too much fat in the diet—especially saturated fat—is linked to numerous cancers, heart disease, and strokes. Most nutritional experts strongly recommend that a person's total fat intake be less than 30 percent of total calories. They also recommended that at least twice as much unsaturated fat as saturated fat be consumed.

Each of the following quantities equals one fat exchange:

*Polyunsaturated Fats*

| | |
|---|---|
| Vegetable oils | 1 teaspoon |
|    Canola | |
|    Corn | |
|    Flax | |
|    Safflower | |
|    Soy | |
|    Sunflower | |
| Avocado (4-inch diameter) | 1/8 |
| Almonds | 10 whole |
| Pecans | 2 large |
| Peanuts | |
|    Spanish | 20 whole |
|    Virginia | 10 whole |
| Seeds | 1 tablespoon |
|    Flax | |
|    Pumpkin | |

Sesame
Sunflower
Walnuts                          6 small

*Monounsaturated Fats*
Olive oil                        1 teaspoon
Olives                           5 small

*Saturated Fats (use sparingly)*
Butter                           1 teaspoon
Bacon                            1 slice
Cream, light or sour             2 tablespoons
Cream, heavy                     1 tablespoon
Cream cheese                     1 tablespoon
Salad dressings                  2 teaspoons
Mayonnaise                       1 teaspoon

## List 6–Milk

Is milk for "everybody"? Definitely not. Many people are allergic to milk or lack the enzymes necessary to digest milk. Drinking cow's milk is a relatively new dietary practice for humans, which may be the reason so many people have difficulty digesting it. Certainly milk consumption should be limited to no more than two servings per day.

For each of the following forms of milk, 1 cup equals one milk exchange:

Nonfat milk or yogurt
2% milk (omit 1 fat exchange)
Low-fat yogurt (omit 1 fat exchange)
Whole milk (omit 2 fat exchanges)
Yogurt (omit 2 fat exchanges)

## List 7–Meats, Fish, Cheese, and Eggs

When choosing from this list, be careful to choose primarily from the low-fat group and to remove the skin of poultry.

This will keep the amount of saturated fat you consume low. Although many people advocate vegetarianism, the following exchange list provides high concentrations of certain nutrients that are difficult to obtain in an entirely vegetarian diet, such as the full range of amino acids, vitamin $B_{12}$, and heme iron. The most important recommendation may be to use these foods in small amounts as "condiments" in the diet rather than as mainstays.

Each of the following quantities equals one meat exchange:

*Low-fat Group (less than 15 percent fat content)*

| | |
|---|---|
| Cottage cheese, low-fat | 1/4 cup |
| Fish | 1 oz |
| Lean beef, veal, or lamb | 1 oz |
| Poultry (chicken or turkey) without skin | 1 oz |

*Medium-fat Group (15 to 20 percent fat content)**

| | |
|---|---|
| Cheese (Mozzarella, ricotta, farmer's, parmesan) | 1 oz |
| Eggs | 1 |
| Beef (hamburger (15 percent fat), organ meats, rib-eye) | 1 oz |

*High-fat Group (more than 20 percent fat)†*

| | |
|---|---|
| Beef (brisket, corned beef, regular hamburger) | 1 oz |
| Cheese (cheddar) | 1 oz |
| Duck or goose | 1 oz |
| Lamb breast | 1 oz |

*Please note that, for each item listed here, you must omit 1/2 fat exchange.
†Please note that, for each item listed here, you must omit 1 fat exchange.

Pork (spareribs, loin,            1 oz
    ground pork,
    country-style ham,
    deviled ham)

## Using the Exchange Lists
## to Design a Healthful Diet

A healthy person's diet should have the following components:

Carbohydrates: 65 to 75 percent of total calories
Fats: 15 to 25 percent of total calories
Protein: 10 to 15 percent of total calories
Dietary fiber: at least 50 grams

Of the carbohydrates ingested, 90 percent should be complex carbohydrates or naturally occurring sugars. Intake of refined carbohydrates and concentrated sugars (including honey, pasteurized fruit juices, dried fruit, refined sugar, and white flour) should be limited to less than 10 percent of total calorie intake. The intake of polyunsaturated fats should be equal to or greater than the intake of saturated fats. Avoiding food components detrimental to health—including sugar, saturated fats, cholesterol, salt, food additives, alcohol, and agricultural residues such as pesticides and herbicides is strongly recommended.

Constructing a diet that meets these recommendations is easy if you use the exchange lists. In addition, these recommendations ensure a high intake of vital whole foods (particularly vegetables) that are rich in nutritional value.

### *Examples of Exchange Recommendations*

*1,500-calorie Vegan Diet*
    List 1–Vegetables: 5 servings

List 2–Fruits: 2 servings
List 3–Breads, Cereals, and Starchy Vegetables: 9 servings
List 4–Legumes: 2 1/2 servings
List 5–Fats and Oils: 4 servings

This recommendation would result in an intake of approximately 1,500 calories, of which 67 percent are derived from complex carbohydrates and naturally occurring sugars, 18 percent from fat, and 15 percent from protein. The protein intake comes entirely from plant sources, but it still provides approximately 55 grams of protein—a number well above the recommended daily amount for someone requiring 1,500 calories. At least half of the fat servings should come from nuts, seeds, and other whole foods from the Fat Exchange List. The dietary fiber intake would be approximately 31 to 74.5 grams.

Percentage of calories as carbohydrates: 67%
Percentage of calories as fats: 18%
Percentage of calories as protein: 15%
Protein content: 55 g
Dietary fiber content: 31 to 74.5 g

*1,500-calorie Omnivore Diet*
List 1–Vegetables: 5 servings
List 2–Fruits: 2 1/2 servings
List 3–Breads, Cereals, and Starchy Vegetables: 6 servings
List 4–Legumes: 1 serving
List 5–Fats and Oils: 5 servings
List 6–Milk: 1 serving
List 7–Meats, Fish, Cheese, and Eggs: 2 servings

Percentage of calories as carbohydrates: 67%
Percentage of calories as fats: 18%
Percentage of calories as protein: 15%

Protein content: 61 g (75% from plant sources)
Dietary fiber content: 19.5 to 53.5 g

*2,000-calorie Vegan Diet*
  List 1–Vegetables: 5 1/2 servings
  List 2–Fruits: 2 servings
  List 3–Breads, Cereals, and Starchy Vegetables: 11
    servings
  List 4–Legumes: 5 servings
  List 5–Fats and Oils: 8 servings

  Percentage of calories as carbohydrates: 67%
  Percentage of calories as fats: 18%
  Percentage of calories as protein: 15%
  Protein content: 79 g
  Dietary fiber content: 48.5 to 101.5 g

*2,000-calorie Omnivore Diet*
  List 1–Vegetables: 5 servings
  List 2–Fruits: 2 1/2 servings
  List 3–Breads, Cereals, and Starchy Vegetables: 13
    servings
  List 4–Legumes: 2 servings
  List 5–Fats and Oils: 7 servings
  List 6–Milk: 1 serving
  List 7–Meats, Fish, Cheese, and Eggs: 2 servings

  Percentage of calories as carbohydrates: 66%
  Percentage of calories as fats: 19%
  Percentage of calories as protein: 15%
  Protein content: 78 g (72% from plant sources)
  Dietary fiber content: 32.5 to 88.5 g

*2,500-calorie Vegan Diet*
  List 1–Vegetables: 8 servings

List 2–Fruits: 3 servings

List 3–Breads, Cereals, and Starchy Vegetables: 17
    servings

List 4–Legumes: 5 servings

List 5–Fats and Oils: 8 servings

Percentage of calories as carbohydrates: 69%

Percentage of calories as fats: 15%

Percentage of calories as protein: 16%

Protein content: 101 g

Dietary fiber content: 33 to 121 g

*2,500-calorie Omnivore Diet*

List 1–Vegetables: 8 servings

List 2–Fruits: 3 1/2 servings

List 3–Breads, Cereals, and Starchy Vegetables: 17
    servings

List 4–Legumes: 2 servings

List 5–Fats and Oils: 8 servings

List 6–Milk: 1 serving

List 7–Meats, Fish, Cheese, and Eggs: 3 servings

Percentage of calories as carbohydrates: 66%

Percentage of calories as fats: 18%

Percentage of calories as protein: 16%

Protein content: 102 g (80% from plant sources)

Dietary fiber content: 40.5 to 116.5 g

*3,000-calorie Vegan Diet*

List 1–Vegetables: 10 servings

List 2–Fruits: 4 servings

List 3–Breads Cereals, and Starchy Vegetables: 17
    servings

List 4–Legumes: 6 servings
List 5–Fats and Oils: 10 servings

Percentage of calories as carbohydrates: 70%
Percentage of calories as fats: 16%
Percentage of calories as protein: 14%
Protein content: 116 g
Dietary fiber content: 50 to 84 g

*3,000-calorie Omnivore Diet*
List 1–Vegetables: 10 servings
List 2–Fruits: 3 servings
List 3–Breads, Cereals, and Starchy Vegetables: 20
    servings
List 4–Legumes: 2 servings
List 5–Fats and Oils: 10 servings
List 6–Milk: 1 serving
List 7–Meats, Fish, Cheese, and Eggs: 3 servings

Percentage of calories as carbohydrates: 67%
Percentage of calories as fats: 18%
Percentage of calories as protein: 15%
Protein content: 116 g (81% from plant sources)
Dietary fiber content: 45 to 133 g

These recommendations can be used as the basis for calculating other-calorie diets. For example, for a 4,000-calorie diet, add the 2,500-calorie diet to the 1,500-calorie diet. For a 1,000-calorie diet, divide the 2,000-calorie diet in half.

## Menu Planning

The Healthy Exchange System was created to enable you to ensure that you are consuming a healthful diet that provides adequate levels of nutrients in their proper ratio. You should begin by determining your caloric needs and calculating the number of servings you need from each Healthy Exchange List. This will help you a great deal when you start constructing a daily menu.

## Breakfast

As discussed in *The Healing Power of Foods,* evaluation of data from the National Health and Nutrition Examination Survey II disclosed that serum cholesterol levels are lowest among adults who eat "ready-to-eat" cereal for breakfast. Although individuals who consumed other breakfast foods had higher blood cholesterol levels, the highest levels of all occurred among adults who typically skipped breakfast. Due to the strong association between cholesterol levels and heart disease, we may conclude from this study that breakfast should be consumed on a regular basis. Breakfast definitely should not be skipped. Furthermore, cereals, both hot and cold (and preferably from whole grains), may be the best food choices for breakfast. The complex carbohydrates in the grains provide sustained energy. Healthful breakfast choices include whole grain cereals, muffins, and breads, along with fresh whole fruit or fresh fruit juice.

## Lunch

Lunch is a great time to enjoy a healthful bowl of soup, a large salad, and some whole-grain bread. Bean soups and other legume dishes are especially good lunch selections for people who have diabetes or other blood-sugar problems, since legumes can markedly improve blood-sugar regulation. Legumes are filling, yet low in calories.

## Snacks

The best snacks are nuts, seeds, fresh fruit, and fresh vegetables (or fresh fruit or vegetable juices).

*Dinner*

For dinner, the most healthful meals contain a fresh vegetable salad, a cooked vegetable side dish or a bowl of soup, whole grains, and legumes. The whole grains may be provided in bread, pasta, or pizza; as a side dish; or as part of a recipe for an entrée. Legumes can be utilized in soups, salads, and entrées.

The recipes in this cookbook do not contain any meat or fish, since a varied diet rich in whole grains, vegetables, and legumes provides optimal levels of protein. Nonetheless, meat, poultry, and fish can be added to many menus or even to the recipes themselves. For example, small amounts of chopped skinless chicken breast can be added to the Stir-fried Vegetables recipe and to other Chinese dishes.

## Constructing a Daily Menu

Earlier, we looked at several examples of how many servings from each Healthy Exchange List could be eaten as part of a healthful diet at several different caloric intake levels. For an example of how to construct a daily menu using these recommendations, let's focus on the specifications for a 2,000-calorie vegan diet (see page 14). Here is a sample menu that would meet these recommendations:

*Breakfast*

    1 serving Happy Apple Breakfast (page 155), with 1 teaspoon butter and 1/2 tablespoon honey

    2 tablespoons pumpkin or sunflower seeds, either mixed with the cereal or eaten separately

    4 ounces fresh orange juice

*Lunch*

    1 serving Insalata Mista Salad (page 80)

    1 serving Lentil Soup (page 54)

    1 slice Dark Peasant Bread (page 97)

*Dinner*
> 1 serving Chinese Bean Salad, with 1 cup sprouted mung
>     beans (page 75)
> 2 servings Four-grain Bread (page 98)
> 1 serving Stir-fried Vegetables (page 138)
> 1 serving Soybean Casserole (page 183)

*Dessert*
> 1 serving Citrus and Mint (page 226)

*Snacks*
> 10 almonds
> 1 glass fresh vegetable juice

Sample Menu

| Exchange List | Breakfast | Lunch | Dinner | Dessert | Snacks |
|---|---|---|---|---|---|
| List 1–Vegetables | | 1 3/4 | 3 | | 1 |
| List 2–Fruits | 1 | 1/4 | | 3/4 | |
| List 3–Breads | 2 | 3 | 6 | | |
| List 4–Legumes | | 1 | 4 | | |
| List 5–Fats and Oils | 3 | 2 | 2 | | 1 |

# The Healing Power of Foods

Thomas Edison believed that "The doctor of the future will give no medicine, but will interest his patient in the care of the human frame, in diet and in the cause and prevention of disease." These are prophetic words, as modern research is confirming that various foods and nutrients act to prevent as well as treat many illnesses. Numerous common medical conditions respond quite well to diet therapy. They respond because appropriate nutrition often addresses the underlying cause of the illness, rather than simply covering up the symptoms.

By following the preceding recommendations for designing

a healthful diet using the Healthy Exchange System, along with eliminating food allergies (see Chapter 13 in *The Healing Power of Foods*), you can help prevent such killers as heart disease, cancer, strokes, and diabetes. In addition, such a diet can be quite therapeutic for most common illnesses. Many common health conditions can be improved further by adopting more specific recommendations. The recommendations that follow summarize key dietary considerations for some of the particular health conditions discussed in greater detail in Chapter 14 of *The Healing Power of Foods*.

These recommendations are intended to serve as general guidelines. They are not designed to substitute for proper medical treatment. In all cases involving a physical or medical complaint, ailment, or therapy, please consult a physician. Proper medical care and advice can significantly improve the quality and duration of your life. For more detailed information on these recommendations, as well as for the supporting references to the medical literature, consult Chapter 14 in *The Healing Power of Foods*.

Although virtually every recipe in this cookbook provides excellent nutritional value and health benefits, the ten suggestions under the "useful recipes" category for each condition discussed provide some key benefits that are highly relevant to that particular condition.

## Acne

*Eliminate consumption of:*
> Refined carbohydrates (sugar and white flour)
> Sources of trans-fatty acids (milk; milk products; margarine, shortening, and other synthetically hydrogenated vegetable oils)
> Fried foods

*Increase consumption of:*
> High-fiber, complex carbohydrate foods such as whole grains, legumes, and vegetables

Foods rich in vitamin A such as carrots, squash, yams, and
dark-green leafy vegetables

Nuts and seeds, for their essential fatty acids and zinc

*Useful recipes:*

Sweet Potato Pumpkin Soup

Jicama Salad

Waldorf Salad

Nut Loaf

Lemon Carrots

Spiced Yams

Black-eyed Peas and Brown Rice

Wild Rice with Mushrooms

Baked Eggplant, Chick-peas and Tomatoes

Spicy Bulgur with Red Beans

## Anemia

*Eliminate consumption of:*

Antagonists of iron absorption such as black tea, coffee,
wheat bran, and egg yolk

*Increase consumption of:*

Green leafy vegetables

Calf liver (4 ounces per day)

Other foods rich in iron (dried beans, blackstrap molasses,
lean meat, organ meats, dried apricots, other dried
fruits, and almonds)

*Useful recipes:*

Lentil Soup

Spinach and Parsnip Soup

Chinese Bean Salad

Country Brussels Sprouts

Greens, Walnuts, and Raisins

Steamed Kale

Black Bean Dal
Homestyle Baked Beans (use blackstrap molasses)
Bean Burritos
Swiss Chard and Garlic with Pasta

## Asthma and Hayfever

*Eliminate consumption of:*
Food allergens
Foods containing additives
All animal products

*Increase consumption of:*
Whole natural foods
Fresh fruits, especially pineapple and berries
Garlic and onions

*Useful recipes:*
Barley Vegetable Soup
Fruit Salad with Maple Dressing
Orange and Fennel Salad
Fennel and Mushrooms
Spicy Hot Leeks
Stir-fried Vegetables
Vegetable Curry
Braised Tempeh Napoletano
Vegetarian Chili
Fruit Combo

## Candidiasis, Chronic

*Eliminate consumption of:*
Simple sugars, including sucrose, fructose, commercial
fruit juices, honey, and maple syrup
Foods with a high content of yeast or mold, including alco-
holic beverages, cheeses, dried fruits, and peanuts

Milk and milk products, due to their high content of lactose (milk sugar) and trace levels of antibiotics

Food allergens

*Increase consumption of:*

High-fiber, complex carbohydrate foods such as whole grains, legumes, and vegetables

Garlic and onions

*Useful recipes:*

Curried Red Lentil Soup

Hummus

Leek and Tomato Casserole

Spicy Hot Leeks

Stuffed Onions

Indian Rice with Pea and Pepper

Polenta Puttanesca

Vegetarian Chili

Spaghetti with Garlic and Hot Pepper

Berry Meringue

## Canker Sores

*Eliminate consumption of:*

Food allergens

Wheat and other sources of gluten

Milk and milk products

*Increase consumption of:*

Green leafy vegetables

High-fiber, complex carbohydrate foods such as whole grains, legumes, and vegetables

*Useful recipes:*

Minestrone

Split Green Pea Soup

Hearty Vegetable Salad

Herbed Green Bean–Zucchini Combo
Vegetables Italiano
Breton Beans
Soybean Casserole
Teriyaki Tofu
Fruit Combo
Melons in a Basket

## Carpal Tunnel Syndrome

*Eliminate consumption of:*
Vitamin $B_6$ antagonists like yellow dye #5 and excessive
protein

*Increase consumption of:*
Foods rich in vitamin $B_6$, including sunflower seeds, soybeans, walnuts, lentils and other legumes, brown
rice, and bananas
Fresh pineapple juice, along with some fresh ginger

*Useful recipes:*
Lentil Soup
Rice, Bean, and Corn Salad
Banana-Oatmeal Pecan Bread
Nut Loaf
Greens, Walnuts, and Raisins
Calico Rice
Gingered Tempeh and Vegetables
Rice with Beans and Vegetables
Soybean Casserole
Bananas in Berry Sauce

## Cataracts

*Eliminate consumption of:*
Fried or grilled foods (sources of damaging free radicals)
Alcohol

*Increase consumption of:*
> Fresh fruits (especially berries) and vegetables, for their antioxidants
>
> High-fiber, complex carbohydrate foods such as whole grains, legumes, and vegetables

*Useful recipes:*
> Sweet Potato Pumpkin Soup
>
> Hearty Vegetable Salad
>
> Insalata Mista
>
> Apple Carrot Muffins
>
> Lemon Carrots
>
> Spiced Yams
>
> Stuffed Onions
>
> Vegetables Italiano
>
> Berry Meringue
>
> Fruit Combo

## Celiac Disease

*Eliminate consumption of:*
> Obvious sources of gluten, especially wheat, barley, oats, and rye
>
> Hidden sources of gluten such as some varieties of soy sauce, modified food starch, ice cream, soup, beer, wine, and alcohol
>
> Food allergens
>
> Milk and milk products

*Increase consumption of:*
> Pineapple
>
> Kiwi fruit
>
> Ginger

*Useful recipes:*
> All recipes that do not have gluten

## Constipation

*Eliminate consumption of:*
> Foods that tend to be constipating, such as milk, cheese, meats, and other low-fiber foods

*Increase consumption of:*
> Whole grains
>
> Breakfast cereals (start with 1/2 cup of bran cereal, increasing to 1 1/2 cups over several weeks)
>
> Prunes

*Useful recipes:*
> Vegetable Rice Salad
>
> Waldorf Salad
>
> Bran Muffins
>
> Four-grain Bread
>
> Greens, Walnuts, and Raisins
>
> Stir-fried Vegetables
>
> Calico Rice
>
> Happy Apple Breakfast
>
> Wild Rice with Mushrooms
>
> Spicy Bulgur with Red Beans

## Diabetes

*Eliminate consumption of:*
> Refined carbohydrates (sugar and white flour)
>
> Processed foods
>
> Quantities of food that cause excess body weight

*Increase consumption of:*
> Foods high in complex carbohydrates, such as vegetables, legumes, and whole grains
>
> Special foods for the diabetic: artichokes, bitter melon, garlic, Jerusalem artichokes, and onions

*Useful recipes:*
> Curried Red Lentil Soup

Lentil Soup
Vegetable Rice Salad
Four-grain Bread
Green Beans Amandine
Medley of Artichokes and Asparagus
Stuffed Onions
Corn and Kidney Bean Pie
Rice with Beans and Vegetables
Vegetarian Chili

## Eczema

*Eliminate consumption of:*
Food allergens (most commonly, cow's milk, eggs, tomatoes, artificial colors, and food preservatives)

*Increase consumption of:*
Flaxseed oil
Coldwater fish such as mackerel, herring, and salmon

*Useful recipes:*
Cold Cucumber and Watercress Soup
Salad Dressings
Hearty Vegetable Salad
Insalata Mista
Vegetable Rice Salad
Cauliflower Creole
Greens, Walnuts, and Raisins
Lemon Carrots
Rice with Beans and Vegetables
Fruit Combo

## Fibrocystic Breast Disease

*Eliminate consumption of:*
Animal products (saturated fats)
Coffee, black tea, and chocolate

*Increase consumption of:*
    High-fiber, complex carbohydrate foods such as whole
        grains, legumes, and vegetables
    Nuts and seeds

*Useful recipes:*
    Lentil Soup
    Rice, Bean, and Corn Salad
    Banana-Oatmeal Pecan Bread
    Nut Loaf
    Greens, Walnuts, and Raisins
    Gingered Tempeh and Vegetables
    Rice with Beans and Vegetables
    Soybean Casserole
    Tofu and Vegetables over Rice
    Bananas in Berry Sauce

## Gallstones

*Eliminate consumption of:*
    Saturated fats and cholesterol
    Quantities of food that produce excess body weight
    Food allergens, especially eggs and pork

*Increase consumption of:*
    High-fiber, complex carbohydrate foods such as whole
        grains, legumes, and vegetables
    Pears, apples, and citrus fruits, for their pectin
    Liquids such as pure water or fresh fruit and vegetable
        juices

*Useful recipes:*
    Italian Bean Soup
    Lentil Soup
    Rice, Bean, and Corn Salad

Old-fashioned Oatmeal Bread
Southern Succotash
Black-eyed Peas and Brown Rice
Happy Apple Breakfast
Corn and Kidney Bean Pie
Baked Apples

## Gout

*Eliminate consumption of:*
Alcohol
High-purine-content foods (organ meats, meat, yeast,
    poultry)
Saturated fats
Refined carbohydrates (sugar and white flour)

*Increase consumption of:*
Flavonoid-rich foods, especially cherries
High-fiber, complex carbohydrate foods such as whole
    grains, legumes, and vegetables
Liquids such as pure water or fresh fruit and vegetable
    juices

*Useful recipes:*
Barley Vegetable Soup
Lentil Salad
Bran Muffins
Four-grain Bread
Stir-fried Vegetables
Vegetable Curry
Calico Rice
Polenta Puttanesca
Vegetarian Chili
Berry Meringue

## Headache (Migraine Type)

*Eliminate consumption of:*

Food allergens (most commonly milk, wheat, chocolate, food additives, tomatoes, and fish)

Wine and beer

*Increase consumption of:*

High-fiber, complex carbohydrate foods such as whole grains, legumes, and vegetables

Fennel and celery

*Useful recipes:*

Barley Vegetable Soup

Borscht

Orange and Fennel Salad

Waldorf Salad

Fennel and Mushrooms

Spicy Hot Leeks

Vegetables Italiano

Vegetable Curry

Rice with Beans and Vegetables

Fruit Combo

## Heart Disease, High Cholesterol Levels, and High Blood Pressure

*Eliminate consumption of:*

Refined carbohydrates (sugar and white flour)

Foods rich in cholesterol and saturated fats (namely, animal products)

Margarine and other sources of hydrogenated oil

Salt

*Increase consumption of:*

High-fiber, complex carbohydrate foods like whole grains, legumes, and vegetables

Nuts and seeds, for their essential fatty acids

High-potassium and high-magnesium foods such as fresh fruit and vegetable juices, bananas, potatoes, whole grains, and nuts

High–vitamin C foods such as broccoli and citrus fruits

Breakfast cereals

Garlic and onions

*Useful recipes:*

Black Bean Soup

Curried Red Lentil Soup

Bran Muffins

Old-fashioned Oatmeal Bread

Vegetable Curry

Happy Apple Breakfast

Hot Cereal

Eggplant Curry

Polenta Puttanesca

Spaghetti with Garlic and Hot Pepper

### Irritable Bowel Syndrome

*Eliminate consumption of:*

Food allergens

Refined carbohydrates (sugar and white flour)

*Increase consumption of:*

High-fiber, complex carbohydrate foods such as whole grains, legumes, and vegetables

Ginger and cinnamon

*Useful recipes:*

Barley Vegetable Soup

Lentil Soup

Vegetable Rice Salad

Waldorf Salad

Apple Carrot Muffins
Spiced Yams
Baked Eggplant, Chick-peas, and Tomatoes
Gingered Tempeh and Vegetables
Rice with Beans and Vegetables
Vegetarian Chili

## Kidney Stones

*Eliminate consumption of:*
Excess protein
High-oxalate foods such as spinach and rhubarb
Salt
Refined carbohydrates
Milk and milk products
Quantities of food that produce excess body weight

*Increase consumption of:*
Fresh fruit and vegetables, especially green leafy vegetables (except spinach)
Liquids such as pure water or fresh fruit and vegetable
juices
High–vitamin $B_6$ and high-magnesium foods such as barley, bran, corn, buckwheat, rye, soy, oats, brown
rice, avocado, banana, lima beans, and potato

*Useful recipes:*
Minestrone
Ratatouille Soup
Insalata Mista
Bran Muffins
Four-grain Bread
Greens, Walnuts, and Raisins
Southern Succotash
Homestyle Baked Beans

Bean Burritos

Bananas with Berry Sauce

## Osteoarthritis

*Eliminate consumption of:*

Quantities of food that produce excess body weight

Nightshade-family vegetables (tomatoes, potatoes, eggplant, peppers, and tobacco)

*Increase consumption of:*

Flavonoid-rich fruits such as cherries, blueberries, and blackberries

Sulfur-containing foods such as legumes, garlic, onions, Brussels sprouts, and cabbage

*Useful recipes:*

Black Bean Soup

Borscht

Chinese Bean Salad

Curried Coleslaw

Vegetable Rice Salad

Green Beans Amandine

Lemon Carrots

Pinto Beans and Corn

Berry Meringue

Fruit Combo

## Osteoporosis

*Eliminate consumption of:*

Refined carbohydrates (sugar and white flour)

Excessive protein

Soft drinks, coffee, and alcohol

*Increase consumption of:*

Foods rich in calcium and vitamin K: kale, spinach, turnip greens, and other green leafy vegetables

Nonfat or low-fat dairy products

*Useful recipes:*
Ratatouille Soup
Insalata Mista
Mediterranean Salad
Orange and Fennel Salad
Banana-Oatmeal Pecan Bread
Nut Loaf
Greens, Walnuts, and Raisins
Steamed Kale
Soybean Casserole
Spring Green Pasta

## Premenstrual Syndrome

*Eliminate consumption of:*
Refined carbohydrates (sugar and white flour)
Milk and milk products
Animal products
Excessive protein
Soft drinks, coffee, chocolate, and alcohol

*Increase consumption of:*
High–vitamin $B_6$ and high-magnesium foods such as barley, bran, corn, buckwheat, rye, soy, oats, brown rice, avocado, banana, lima beans, and potato
Nuts and seeds

*Useful recipes:*
Curried Red Lentil Soup
Rice, Bean, and Corn Salad
Banana-Oatmeal Pecan Bread
Nut Loaf
Fennel and Mushrooms
Greens, Walnuts, and Raisins
Gingered Tempeh and Vegetables

Rice with Beans and Vegetables
Soybean Casserole
Bananas in Berry Sauce

### Prostate Enlargement (BPH)

*Eliminate consumption of:*
Foods high in cholesterol and saturated fats
Beer

*Increase consumption of:*
Nuts and seeds, for their zinc and essential fatty acids
Pumpkin seeds

*Useful recipes:*
Curried Red Lentil Soup
Sunflower Salad Dressing
Insalata Mista
Four-grain Bread
Nut Loaf
Old-fashioned Oatmeal Bread
Sunflower Power Cookies
Greens, Walnuts, and Raisins
Soybean Casserole
Stuffed Peaches with Fresh Cherries and Almonds

### Psoriasis

*Eliminate consumption of:*
Animal products (except coldwater fish)
Refined carbohydrates (sugar and white flour)
Alcohol

*Increase consumption of:*
High-fiber, complex carbohydrate foods such as legumes,
whole grains, and vegetables
Flaxseed oil

*Useful recipes:*
Borscht
Curried Red Lentil Soup
Vegetable Rice Salad
Four-grain Bread
Vegetable Curry
Breton Beans
Wild Rice with Mushrooms
Mexican Polenta Pie
Tofu and Vegetables over Rice
Spaghetti with Garlic and Hot Pepper

## Rheumatoid Arthritis

*Eliminate consumption of:*
Animal products
Food allergens, most commonly wheat, corn, milk and other dairy products, beef, and nightshade-family foods (tomato, potato, eggplants, peppers, and tobacco)
Refined carbohydrates (sugar and white flour)

*Increase consumption of:*
High-fiber, complex carbohydrate foods such as legumes, whole grains, and vegetables
Cold-water fish such as mackerel, herring, sardines, and salmon, or flaxseed oil
Fresh fruit and vegetable juices
Cherries, berries, and citrus fruits
Fresh pineapple
Ginger, garlic, and onions

*Useful recipes:*
Barley Vegetable Soup
Sweet Potato Pumpkin Soup

Jicama Salad (omit bell pepper)
Orange and Fennel Salad
Spiced Yams
Black Bean Dal
Black-eyed Peas and Brown Rice
Teriyaki Tofu
Citrus and Mint
Fruit Combo

## Ulcer

*Eliminate consumption of:*
Milk and milk products
Alcohol
Refined carbohydrates (sugar and white flour)
Food allergens

*Increase consumption of:*
High-fiber, complex carbohydrate foods such as legumes,
    whole grains, and vegetables
Fresh cabbage juice
Cabbage, broccoli, cauliflower, and other cabbage-family
    vegetables

*Useful recipes:*
No-Cream of Broccoli Soup
Curried Coleslaw
Cauliflower Creole
Country Brussels Sprouts
Breton Beans
Rice with Beans and Vegetables
Tofu and Vegetables over Rice
Swiss Chard and Garlic with Pasta
Baked Apples
Plantain Patties

## *Varicose Veins*

*Eliminate consumption of:*
> Refined carbohydrates (sugar and white flour)
> Foods high in cholesterol and saturated fats

*Increase consumption of:*
> High-fiber, complex carbohydrate foods such as legumes, whole grains, and vegetables
> Flavonoid-rich fruit such as cherries, blueberries, currants, blackberries, and citrus fruits
> Fresh pineapple
> Ginger, red peppers, garlic, and onions

*Useful recipes:*
> Citrus and Fennel Salad
> Vegetable Rice Salad
> Bran Muffins
> Four-grain Bread
> Happy Apple Breakfast
> Curried Vegetables
> Polenta Puttanesca
> Wild Rice with Mushrooms
> Bananas in Berry Sauce
> Citrus and Mint

## Final Comments

Meals are excellent times to give thanks for all that you may have. Many people throughout the world are not so fortunate. Somehow, acknowledging this greatly increases the enjoyment of any meal. Eating is truly a celebration of life, so make sure that your meals are designed to contribute to a healthy life.

# 2

## ····*Setting Up a Healthful Kitchen*

Cooking for health means increasing your reliance on foods you prepare yourself. A well-equipped kitchen will make this task much easier and more enjoyable. For example, a food processor is an invaluable appliance that will save much time and effort over cutting, chopping, grinding, or mixing by hand. This chapter presents a list of some absolute necessities to have in your kitchen, followed by a list of accessory items.

## Necessities

*Pots and Pans*   High-quality pots and pans can be expensive, but you usually get what you pay for. Avoid aluminum-lined pots and pans, due to the possible link between aluminum and Alzheimer's disease. Nonstick frying pans will reduce the amount of oil or butter required in cooking. The following pots and pans are recommended; all should have tight-fitting lids and ovenproof handles:

    1-quart sauce pan
    2-quart sauce pan

5-quart saucepot
8-quart stock pot
8-inch nonstick frying pan
10-inch nonstick frying pan
3-quart casserole dish
glass baking dish, 13 × 9 × 2 inches
loaf pans (two), 9 × 5 × 3 inches
baking sheet, 18 × 12 × 1 inch
12-inch pizza pan

*Wok*  The wok may be electric or it may be designed to be placed over the heating element on your stove. Again, a non-stick surface will reduce the need for oil or butter, thereby reducing calories.

*Blender*  The more powerful the motor on the blender, the longer it will last and the better it will serve. Choose one that has at least five different speed settings.

*Knives*  A good set of knives is essential. Your set should include the following items:

two paring knives
one cook's knife, 6 inches long
one chef's knife, 8 inches long
one serrated bread knife, 8 inches long

*Cutting Board*  Acrylic or plastic cutting boards are the most durable and the most sanitary.

*Utensils*  The following utensils are necessary in a health-oriented kitchen:

Can opener
Colander
Garlic press

Grater (four-sided)
Measuring cups and spoons
Mixing bowl set
Mixing spoons
Mortar and pestle
Salad spinner
Soup ladle
Spatulas (one rubber and three wooden)
Strainer
Tongs
Vegetable peeler
Vegetable steamer
Wire whisk
Wooden spoons (three)

## Accessories

The following items, although not necessities, will certainly make cooking a lot easier and more enjoyable.

*Bread Baker*   This may very well be the most labor-saving of all home appliances. An automatic bread baker does all the work for you. All you do is mix the ingredients together and pour the mixture into the machine. The machine takes care of the kneading and the baking.

*Crock Pot*   There are two major types of crock pots: continuous slow-cookers, and cookers whose heating element cycles on and off. Continuous cookers are the preferred type. Crock pots are fantastic for preparing legume dishes.

*Flour Mill*   Grinding your own whole grains to produce fresh flour enables you to obtain nutritional benefits superior to those of store-bought flours.

*Food Dehydrator* Dehydrating fruits and vegetables lets you turn them into delicious and highly nutritious snacks.

*Food Processor* The food processor has become the most popular kitchen appliance because of its versatility. Although many of the functions it performs can be performed by hand, it is definitely worth the investment.

*Juice Extractor* It is hard to imagine anyone committed to health not having a high-quality juice extractor in the kitchen.

*Pasta Maker* Fresh homemade pasta is a fantastic way to increase your consumption of whole grains.

*Pressure Cooker* A pressure cooker dramatically reduces the time required for cooking grains and legumes. Since the New Four Food Groups lists focus on these foods, many health-conscious people really appreciate the pressure cooker.

*Rice Cooker* Select a rice cooker that has a special cycle on it for cooking brown rice. Most rice cookers have automatic cooking features and timers. Another useful feature is an electric microprocessor that monitors the appliance's internal temperature and moisture. This enables the rice to stay warm and moist for up to 12 hours.

*Toaster or Toaster Oven* Fresh toast is a morning ritual for many, and a toaster is found in nearly every kitchen in America.

# 3

## ••••Soups

Soups are a great way to start off a delicious meal, especially during the cooler months of fall and winter. Soups are also great as a lunch; and some of the heartier soups, such as those containing legumes, can also serve as dinner entrées. Combining some whole-grain bread with a legume-based soup produces a complete-protein meal.

## ••••Vegetable Stock

*Makes 4 Servings*

| | |
|---|---|
| 1/2 | cup chopped onion |
| 1 | clove garlic |
| 1/2 | cup diced carrots |
| 1/2 | cup diced turnip or parsnip |
| 1 | cup diced celery ribs, plus several whole leaves |
| 1 | cup potato peelings, mushroom bits, shredded salad greens, or vegetable scraps |
| 3 | sprigs fresh parsley |

| | |
|---|---|
| 2 | whole cloves |
| 1 | bay leaf |
| 1/2 | teaspoon thyme |
| 1/2 | teaspoon black pepper |
| 1/2 | teaspoon Lite Salt or salt substitute |
| | Cayenne pepper to taste |
| 3 | quarts water |

Combine all the ingredients in a soup pot, and bring to a boil. Reduce heat and simmer, partially covered, for approximately 1 1/2 hours. Then pour the stock through a fine strainer, sieve, or cheesecloth into a suitable container, pressing the solids to extract all the liquid. The solids can then be discarded.

*Exchanges per Serving:*
Vegetables: 1

*Nutritional Information per Serving:*
Calories: 56
Carbohydrate: 79%
Protein: 13%
Fat: 8%
Fiber: 2 g
Calcium: 50 mg

*Comments:* This versatile vegetable stock recipe can serve as a general guideline for creating your own special recipe.

◆◆◆◆

# ···· *Barley Vegetable Soup*

*Makes 6 Servings*

| | |
|---|---|
| 1/4 | cup washed whole barley |
| 6 | cups boiling vegetable stock |
| 1 | cup sliced carrots |
| 1/2 | cup diced celery |
| 1/4 | cup chopped onions |
| 2 | cups skinned, chopped tomatoes |
| 1 | cup fresh (or frozen) peas |
| 1/2 | cup chopped parsley |
| | Lite Salt or salt substitute to taste |

Place the barley and stock in a heavy kettle, cover, and simmer until the barley is tender. This usually takes about 1 hour. Add the remaining ingredients, except the parsley, and cook, covered, until the vegetables are barely tender. Remove from heat and add the parsley.

*Exchanges per Serving:*
Vegetables: 2
Grains and starches: 1/2
Legumes: 1/3

*Nutritional Information per Serving:*

| Calories: 186 | Protein: 10% | Fiber: 5 g |
|---|---|---|
| Carbohydrate: 70% | Fat: 20% | Calcium: 98 mg |

*Comments:* A hearty soup, especially warming after outdoor activity on a brisk fall day.

♦ ♦ ♦ ♦

# ••••*Black Bean Soup*

*Makes 4 Servings*

|  |  |
|---|---|
| 2 | teaspoons extra-virgin olive oil or canola oil |
| 2 | medium red onions, chopped |
| 1 | jalapeño chile, minced |
| 2 | large garlic cloves, minced |
| 1 | teaspoon ground cumin |
| 1/2 | teaspoon chili powder |
| 4 | cups cooked black beans |
| 2 | cups water |
| 2 | tablespoons sour cream (optional) |

In a medium saucepan, heat the olive oil. Add the chopped onion and minced jalapeño, and cook over moderate heat, stirring frequently, until the onion begins to brown, about 4 minutes. Stir in the garlic, reduce the heat to low, and cook, stirring constantly, for 1 minute. Stir in the cumin and chili powder. Combine the spice mixture, water, and beans in a heavy pot. Cook over low heat, stirring occasionally, until the beans are hot, about 5 minutes. If a smooth texture is preferred, transfer the soup to a food processor or blender and purée until smooth.

*Exchanges per Serving:*
Vegetables: 1          Legumes: 2          Fats: 1/2

*Nutritional Information per Serving:*
Calories: 248          Protein: 19%          Fiber: 22 g
Carbohydrate: 65%          Fat: 16%          Calcium: 137 mg

*Comments:* This soup can be made up to 4 days ahead; simply pour it into an air-tight container, refrigerate, and reheat when wanted.

••••

# ···· *Borscht*

*Makes 4–6 Servings*

| | |
|---|---|
| 8 | medium beets (peeled and grated) with tops (finely chopped) |
| 1 | small onion |
| 2 | quarts homemade vegetable stock |
| | Juice of 1 lemon |
| 1/4 | teaspoon paprika |
| 1/2 | teaspoon fresh dill |

In a soup pot, combine beets, onion, and vegetable stock. Bring to a boil; then reduce heat to medium low and simmer until vegetables are well cooked. Add lemon juice and beet tops and cook 5 to 10 minutes more. Season with paprika and dill.

**Exchanges per Serving:**
Vegetables: 1 1/2

**Nutritional Information per Serving:**
Calories: 63
Carbohydrate: 78%
Protein: 19%
Fat: 3%
Fiber: 2 g
Calcium: 102 mg

**Comments:** This simple soup is a Russian classic for good reason; it is nutritious and delicious.

◆◆◆◆

# ••••Carrot and Parsnip Soup with Vegetables

*Makes 8 Servings*

| | |
|---|---|
| 6 | medium carrots, chopped |
| 1 | large parsnip, chopped |
| 1 | small onion, chopped |
| 3 | cups water |
| 2 | cloves garlic, minced |
| 1 | cup chopped broccoli |
| 1 | cup chopped asparagus |
| 1 | cup chopped zucchini |
| 1 | cup fresh (or frozen) peas |
| 1 | sprig fresh parsley, finely chopped |
| 1 | teaspoon cumin |
| 1 | teaspoon sweet marjoram |
| 1 | teaspoon dried basil |
| 1/2 | teaspoon white pepper |
| 1/2 | teaspoon allspice |
| 1/2 | teaspoon cinnamon |

In a soup pot, cook carrots, parsnip, onion, and garlic in the water until very tender. Purée or mash; then return to medium heat, adding water if the mixture is too thick. Add the remaining ingredients to the purée mixture and cook until tender, but not mushy. Add spices to taste.

**Exchanges per Serving:**
Vegetables: 1 1/2

**Nutritional Information per Serving:**

| | | |
|---|---|---|
| Calories: 75 | Protein: 11% | Fiber: 2 g |
| Carbohydrate: 84% | Fat: 5% | Calcium: 50 mg |

*Comments:* By combining several highly nutrient-dense vegetables, this soup provides a wide range of nutrients, but relatively few calories.

◆◆◆◆

# ••••*Cauliflower and Pasta Soup*

*Makes 6 Servings*

| | |
|---|---|
| 1 | tablespoon olive oil |
| 4 | cloves minced garlic |
| 2 | medium onions, diced |
| 2 | tablespoons tomato paste |
| 10 | cups vegetable stock |
| 1 | tablespoon soy sauce |
| 1 | bay leaf |
| 1/3 | teaspoon oregano |
| 1/4 | teaspoon basil |
| 1/4 | teaspoon thyme |
| 1 | teaspoon Lite Salt or salt substitute |
| | Freshly ground pepper |
| 1 | large cauliflower |
| 1 | cup macaroni or other small pasta |
| 1/4 | cup minced fresh parsley |

In a large stockpot over medium heat, heat the olive oil. Add the garlic and onions, and cook for 10 minutes, stirring often. Add the tomato paste, and cook for 1 minute. Add the vegetable stock, soy sauce, herbs, salt, and pepper, and bring to a boil. Cut the cauliflower into bite-size pieces, and add to the boiling soup. Add the macaroni and bring to a boil again. Cook for 20 minutes over reduced heat until tender.

*Exchanges per Serving:*
Vegetables: 1
Grains and starches: 1/2
Fats: 1/2

*Nutritional Information per Serving:*
Calories: 95
Carbohydrate: 65%
Protein: 14%
Fat: 21%
Fiber: 4 g
Calcium: 179 mg

*Comments:* This soup is quite filling and satisfying.

◆◆◆◆

# ◆◆◆◆ Cold Cucumber and Watercress Soup

*Makes 4–6 Servings*

| | |
|---|---|
| 1 | tablespoon canola oil |
| 2 | medium onions |
| 3 | large cucumbers (halved and sliced into 1/2-inch chunks) |
| 2 | cups vegetable stock |
| 2 | teaspoons fresh tarragon |
| 1/2 | teaspoon vinegar |
| 1/4 | teaspoon Lite Salt or salt substitute |
| | Ground black pepper |
| 1 | bunch watercress |

In a medium-size saucepan, sauté the onions in the canola oil. Add the sliced cucumber, vegetable stock, vinegar, salt, and pepper. Cover the pot and bring to a boil. Cook over medium heat for 20 minutes or until the cucumbers are tender. Wash the watercress and mince the leaves. When the cucumbers are very tender, purée the soup in a blender or food processor. Pour the soup into a large bowl, stir in the minced watercress, and chill for at least 3 hours. Serve cold.

*Exchanges per Serving:*
Vegetables: 1
Fats: 3/4

*Nutritional Information per Serving:*
Calories: 85
Carbohydrate: 52%
Protein: 19%
Fat: 29%
Fiber: 2 g
Calcium: 219 mg

*Comments:* This cool, refreshing soup tastes best during the summer.

◆◆◆◆

# ···· *Curried Red Lentil Soup*

*Makes 4 Servings*

| | |
|---|---|
| 1 1/2 | cups red lentils |
| 4 | cups water |
| 1 | tablespoon olive oil |
| 1/2 | teaspoon Lite Salt or salt substitute |
| 2 | medium potatoes, diced |
| 1 | medium onion, chopped |
| 2 | cloves garlic, minced |
| 1 | teaspoon turmeric |
| 1 | teaspoon ground cumin |
| 1 | teaspoon ground coriander |
| 1/2 | teaspoon cayenne pepper |

Rinse the lentils in a strainer with cold running water. Combine lentils, water, oil, and salt in a medium saucepan. Bring to a boil and cook uncovered for 20 minutes over medium heat. Stir occasionally. Add the diced potatoes and stir. In a small skillet, heat the vegetable oil. Add the onion, garlic, and spices. Cook until onions begin to get tender. Add the onions, garlic, and spices to the soup, and cook until the potatoes are tender. This will take about 20 minutes.

*Exchanges per Serving:*
Vegetables: 1                 Legumes: 1
Grains and starches: 1/2      Fats: 3/4

*Nutritional Information per Serving:*
Calories: 196        Protein: 14%     Fiber: 4 g
Carbohydrate: 77%    Fat: 9%          Calcium: 60 mg

*Comments:* This is a great soup for a person who has diabetes, high blood pressure, or elevated cholesterol levels.

◆◆◆◆

# ••••*Italian Bean Soup*

*Makes 4 Servings*

| | |
|---|---|
| 2 | cups dried white kidney beans or other white beans, soaked overnight |
| 1 | bay leaf |
| 1 | teaspoon Lite Salt or salt substitute |
| 1/3 | cup olive oil |
| 1 | clove of garlic |
| 1/2 | cup chopped fresh parsley |
| 1/2 | teaspoon freshly ground black pepper |
| 1 | tablespoon cider vinegar (optional) |
| 4 | slices whole wheat bread, toasted |

Rinse and drain the beans, put them in a large saucepan with the bay leaf and cover with cold water. Add the salt, bring to boil, and then simmer gently, covered, for about 1 1/2–2 hours or until the beans are tender. Drain the beans and re-serve 2 cups of the cooking liquid. Heat the olive oil in a large saucepan, and cook the garlic until just lightly colored. Add the parsley, beans, and reserved bean liquid. Simmer for a few minutes. Season with freshly ground black pepper and cider vinegar, if used. Serve over slices of toasted whole wheat bread.

**Exchanges per Serving:**
Grains and starches: 1    Legumes: 2        Fats: 3/4

**Nutritional Information per Serving:**
Calories: 275            Protein: 15%        Fiber: 14 g
Carbohydrate: 65%        Fat: 20%            Calcium: 88 mg

**Comments:** This high-fiber soup makes an excellent lunch.

••••

# ••••*Lentil Soup*

*Makes 6 Servings*

|  |  |
|---|---|
| 1 | tablespoon olive oil |
| 2 | large onions, finely diced |
| 4 | cloves garlic, minced |
| 2 | green peppers, finely diced |
| 10 | cups vegetable stock, homemade or store-bought |
| 2 | carrots, thinly sliced |
| 1 1/2 | cups lentils, picked over and rinsed |
| 1/3 | teaspoon thyme |
|  | Liberal seasoning with freshly ground pepper |
| 1/2 | teaspoon Lite Salt or salt substitute |
|  | 28-ounce can imported plum tomatoes in their juice, finely chopped |
| 1 | pound loose fresh spinach (stems removed), finely chopped; or 10-ounce package frozen chopped spinach, thawed |

Heat the oil in a large stockpot over medium heat. Add the onions, garlic, and green peppers, and sauté for 10 minutes. Add all of the remaining ingredients except the spinach, and bring to a boil. Reduce the heat to a simmer, and cook, stirring occasionally, for 45 minutes or until the lentils are tender. Add the chopped spinach and cook for 5 more minutes, or until it has wilted and become tender. Taste to adjust the seasoning.

*Exchanges per Serving:*
Vegetables: 1
Legumes: 1
Fats: 1/2

*Nutritional Information per Serving:*
Calories: 182
Carbohydrate: 54%
Protein: 16%
Fat: 30%
Fiber: 2 g
Calcium: 137 mg

*Comments:* Served with bread, this soup provides excellent protein.

◆◆◆◆

# ◆◆◆◆ *Minestrone*

*Makes 4 Servings*

| | |
|---|---|
| 1 | onion, finely chopped |
| 1 | cup finely chopped celery |
| 2 | medium tomatoes, chopped (reserve juice) |
| 1/2 | cup chopped fresh parsley |
| 2 | dried bay leaves |
| 2 | teaspoons dried basil |
| 1/2 | teaspoon rosemary |
| 1/2 | clove garlic |
| 1 | cup mixed vegetables (chopped carrots, zucchini, broccoli, green peas, green beans, green bell pepper, cabbage, and mushrooms) |
| 3 | cups homemade vegetable stock |

In a soup pot, combine all the ingredients and bring to a boil. Then reduce heat to medium low, and simmer until the vegetables are tender.

*Exchanges per Serving:*
Vegetables: 1

*Nutritional Information per Serving:*

| | |
|---|---|
| Calories: 56 | Fat: 9% |
| Carbohydrate: 75% | Fiber: 2 g |
| Protein: 16% | Calcium: 140 mg |

*Comments:* A high-potassium soup, and a great way to start off any meal.

◆◆◆◆

# ◆◆◆◆ *No-Cream of Broccoli Soup*

*Makes 2 Servings*

| | |
|---|---|
| 1 | medium onion, sliced |
| 1 | medium carrot, sliced |
| 1 | stalk celery, sliced |
| 1 | clove garlic |
| 1 | cup vegetable broth or water |
| 2 | cups broccoli, chopped |
| 1/2 | cup macaroni |
| 1 | cup 1% soymilk (or nonfat milk) |
| | Generous pinch of cayenne pepper and grated ginger |
| 1/2 | teaspoon Lite Salt or salt substitute |

Cover and simmer onion, carrot, celery, garlic, and vegetable broth for 5 minutes. Add broccoli and pasta, and simmer another 5–10 minutes. Transfer to blender; add soymilk, cayenne pepper, and salt; purée.

*Exchanges per Serving:*
Vegetables: 1
Grains and starches: 1/2
Milk: 1/2

*Nutritional Information per Serving:*
Calories: 144
Carbohydrate: 65%
Protein: 26%
Fat: 9%
Fiber: 3 g
Calcium: 257 mg

*Comments:* A healthful alternative to cream-based versions.

◆◆◆◆

# ····*Pumpkin Bisque*

*Makes 4 Servings*

|   |   |
|---|---|
| 1 | small pumpkin (about 2 1/2 pounds) |
| 2 | tablespoons canola oil |
| 1 | carrot, grated |
| 2 | medium onions |
| 1 | clove garlic, minced |
| 1/4 | teaspoon Lite Salt or salt substitute |
| 5 | cups vegetable stock |
|   | Dash of cayenne pepper |
| 1 | tomato |

Slice off the top and bottom of the pumpkin and set it upright. From top to bottom, cut off the skin as you would cut off the peel of an orange. Cut the pumpkin in half, and scoop out the seeds. Cut the pumpkin into 1 1/2-inch chunks. In a saucepan, heat the vegetable oil and add the carrot, onions, and garlic. Cook for 10 minutes. Add the pumpkin, salt, vegetable stock, and cayenne pepper; cover the pan and bring to a boil. Drop the whole tomato in for 30 seconds, then remove. Peel off the skin and discard it. Cut the tomato in half horizontally, and then squeeze out the seeds. Mince the tomato and add it to the soup. Reduce the heat and simmer for 30 minutes uncovered. Remove from heat and purée the soup in a blender or food processor until very smooth. Return the soup to the pot and reheat.

*Exchanges per Serving:*
Vegetables: 1
Grains and starches: 1
Fats: 1 1/2

*Nutritional Information per Serving:*
Calories: 193
Carbohydrate: 68%
Protein: 10%
Fat: 22%
Fiber: 7 g
Calcium: 156 mg

*Comments:* If you like pumpkin, you'll love this soup.

◆◆◆◆

# ••••*Quick Tomato-Rice Soup*

*Makes 4 Servings*

> **10-ounce can tomato soup**
> 2 1/2 **cups vegetable broth**
> 1 **cup brown rice**
> 3/4 **cup finely chopped celery**

Combine soup, broth, rice, celery, and pepper. Bring to a boil, and then reduce heat. Cover and simmer for 20 minutes or until the rice is tender.

*Exchanges per Serving:*
Vegetables: 1
Grains and starches: 1

*Nutritional Information per Serving:*
Calories: 122
Carbohydrate: 70%
Protein: 17%
Fat: 13%
Fiber: 0.6 g
Calcium: 19.5 mg

*Comments:* This soup is quick and easy.

••••

# ••••*Ratatouille Soup*

*Makes 4 Servings*

| | |
|---|---|
| 1 | pound tomatoes, chopped |
| 1 | onion, chopped |
| 1 | green bell pepper, chopped |
| 2 | cloves garlic, minced |
| 2 | bay leaves |
| 1 | eggplant, chopped (do not peel) |
| 1 | teaspoon dried basil |
| 1 | teaspoon marjoram |
| 1/2 | teaspoon dried oregano |
| 1/2 | teaspoon rosemary |
| 1/4 | cup chopped fresh parsley |

In a soup pot, cook the tomatoes, onion, green pepper, garlic, and bay leaves until almost tender. If the mixture is too thick, add low-sodium tomato juice or water. Add eggplant, basil, marjoram, oregano, and rosemary to the pot, and cook until the eggplant and other ingredients are tender. Add the parsley, and heat through. Remove the bay leaves before serving. This soup is good hot or cold.

**Exchanges per Serving:**
Vegetables: 1 1/2

**Nutritional Information per Serving:**

| | | |
|---|---|---|
| Calories: 79 | Protein: 14% | Fiber: 2 g |
| Carbohydrate: 77% | Fat: 9% | Calcium: 98 mg |

**Comments:** A highly nutritious soup that is especially useful for lowering cholesterol levels, because of the garlic and eggplant.

••••

# •••• *Spinach and Parsnip Soup*

*Makes 4 Servings*

- 2 **cups water**
- 3 **medium parsnips, chopped**
- 1 **small onion, chopped**
- 1 **bunch fresh spinach, finely chopped; or 1 package frozen spinach**
- 1 **cup chopped mushrooms**
- 1 **tablespoon curry powder**
- 1 **teaspoon chervil**
- 1/2 **teaspoon cinnamon**
- 1/4 **cup fresh parsley**

In a soup pot, cook the parsnips and onion in the water until very tender. Mash or purée in a blender. Return to heat. If the mixture is too thick, add more water. In another saucepan, cook the spinach and mushrooms until very tender. Mash or purée in a blender, and pour into the parsnip mixture. Add herbs and spices to taste. The parsnips make this a little sweet, and if the spinach and mushrooms are finely chopped, the soup will be very smooth. If the soup is too thick, add water. The flavor mellows with reheating.

*Exchanges per Serving:*
Vegetables: 2

*Nutritional Information per Serving:*

| | | |
|---|---|---|
| Calories: 103 | Protein: 13% | Fiber: 15 g |
| Carbohydrate: 81% | Fat: 6% | Calcium: 140 mg |

*Comments:* A nutrient-dense soup that is an especially good source of calcium.

••••

# ••••*Split Green Pea Soup*

*Makes 6 Servings*

| | |
|---|---|
| 10 | cups vegetable stock |
| 2 | cups split green peas, washed and drained |
| 1 | tablespoon olive oil |
| 1 | large onion, finely chopped |
| 1 | celery stalk, finely chopped |
| 1 | large carrot, finely chopped |
| | Lite Salt or salt substitute and freshly ground black pepper |

Bring the stock to a boil. Add the split peas; cover and simmer over low heat for about 30 minutes. In a second pan, heat the oil; add the chopped onion, celery, and carrot; and cook covered for about 15 minutes, until the vegetables have softened. Add the softened vegetables to the stock and split peas. Season with salt and freshly ground black pepper; cover and simmer gently for 45–60 more minutes. Stir occasionally to prevent the soup from sticking to the pan. Purée in a blender. Return to the saucepan, and bring slowly to a boil. If the soup seems too thick, add some water; if too thin boil uncovered until the correct consistency is obtained. Taste the soup and adjust the seasoning.

*Exchanges per Serving:*

| | | |
|---|---|---|
| Vegetables: 1 | Legumes: 1 | Fats: 1/2 |

*Nutritional Information per Serving:*

| | | |
|---|---|---|
| Calories: 160 | Protein: 12% | Fiber: 6 g |
| Carbohydrate: 59% | Fat: 29% | Calcium: 119 mg |

**Comments:** A great way to increase the nutritional quality of a grain-based meal.

••••

# ••••Sweet Potato Pumpkin Soup

*Makes 8 Servings*

| | |
|---|---|
| 1/2 | quart peeled sweet potatoes, cut into chunks |
| 1/2 | quart peeled pumpkin, cut into chunks |
| 3 | cups thickly sliced leeks or onions |
| 3 | carrots, cut into chunks |
| 3 | ribs celery, sliced into large chunks |
| 2 | quarts water |
| 1 | teaspoon Lite Salt or salt substitute |
| 1/2 | teaspoon freshly ground pepper |
| 1 | tablespoon vegetable oil |
| 2 | tablespoons toasted sesame seeds |
| 1 | tablespoon caraway seeds |
| 2 | teaspoons chopped fresh tarragon or 1/2 teaspoon dried tarragon |

Place the sweet potatoes, pumpkin, leeks, carrots, celery, and water in a large kettle. Add salt and pepper. Bring to a boil, cover, and simmer for 40 minutes. The soup will be lumpy. With a slotted spoon, remove and reserve half of the carrots and celery and some firmer potato chunks. Purée the remainder of the soup in a food mill or electric blender until smooth. Return this to the kettle, and add the oil, sesame seeds, caraway seeds, and tarragon. Reheat, check taste, and add extra salt or pepper if desired. Serve immediately.

**Exchanges per Serving:**
Vegetables: 1 1/2
Fats: 3/4

**Nutritional Information per Serving:**

| | | |
|---|---|---|
| Calories: 112 | Protein: 9% | Fiber: 4 g |
| Carbohydrate: 70% | Fat: 21% | Calcium: 52 mg |

*Comments:* A soup rich in beta-carotene and other substances protective against cancer.

◆◆◆◆

# ◆◆◆◆ *Tomato Soup*

*Makes 4 Servings*

|       |                                      |
|-------|--------------------------------------|
| 3     | cups finely chopped fresh tomatoes   |
| 1     | medium onion, finely chopped         |
| 2     | stalks celery, finely chopped        |
| 1     | large carrot, grated                 |
| 1     | quart homemade vegetable stock       |
| 3/4   | teaspoon dried oregano               |
| 1 1/2 | teaspoons dried basil                |
|       | Black pepper to taste                |

In a soup pot, add the tomatoes, onion, celery, and carrot to vegetable stock. Bring to a boil, and then reduce heat to medium low. Add seasonings and simmer until the vegetables are tender.

**Exchanges per Serving:**
Vegetables: 1

**Nutritional Information per Serving:**

| | | |
|---|---|---|
| Calories: 62 | Protein: 15% | Fiber: 1.5 g |
| Carbohydrate: 77% | Fat: 9% | Calcium: 85 mg |

*Comments:* A light soup that is perfect with a heavier meal.

◆◆◆◆

# 4

## ••••Salad Dressings and Salads

The importance of eating fresh salads on a regular basis cannot be overstated. Fresh fruits and vegetables are nutritionally superior in their uncooked state. Salads must become a big part of your diet, especially if you are trying to lose a few pounds. Eating the same type of salad day after day can become a bit monotonous so it is important to vary the types of salads and salad dressings you eat. The salad dressings presented here lend variety to even a simple green salad. The salads that follow offer a wide range of delicious flavors and textures.

## ◆ Salad Dressings ◆

Most commercially available salad dressings, including those served in restaurants, are full of the wrong type of fats and oils. The salad dressings described in this section are fantastic in providing your body with the types of oils that it needs to maintain or achieve health. These oils are particularly important in fighting heart disease, tissue inflammation, and possibly even cancer. Salad dressings are the perfect opportunity to use polyunsaturated and therapeutic vegetable oils such as flaxseed, safflower, sunflower, and soy.

# ••••Basil Dressing

*Makes 6 Servings (2 tablespoons per serving)*

| | |
|---|---|
| 1/4 | cup vegetable oil |
| 3 | tablespoons fresh lemon juice |
| 1/4 | cup water |
| 2 | tablespoons minced fresh basil or 1 1/2 teaspoons dried basil |
| 1 | teaspoon finely chopped garlic |
| | Black pepper to taste |

Combine all of the ingredients in a blender or food processor, and mix thoroughly.

**Exchanges per Serving:**
Fats: 2

**Nutritional Information per Serving:**
Calories: 56
Carbohydrate: 5%
Protein: 1%
Fat: 93%
Fiber: trace
Calcium: 7 mg

◆◆◆◆

# ••••*Dijon Salad Dressing*

*Makes 8 Servings (2 tablespoons per serving)*

| | |
|---|---|
| 3 | tablespoons dijon mustard (prepared) |
| 3 | tablespoons apple cider vinegar |
| 6 | tablespoons water |
| 3/4 | cup vegetable oil |
| 1/4 | teaspoon Lite Salt or salt substitute |
| 1/4 | teaspoon freshly ground black pepper |
| 1 | teaspoon fresh herbs (chives, basil, parsley, chopped) |

Combine all of the ingredients in a small bowl, and mix well with a fork. When they are thoroughly mixed, chill for 1 hour. This dressing will keep for 1 week.

*Exchanges per Serving:*
Fats: 3

*Nutritional Information per Serving:*
Calories: 185
Carbohydrate: 13%
Protein: 5%
Fat: 82%
Fiber: trace
Calcium: 19 mg

••••

# ••••*Herb Dressing*

*Makes 8 Servings (2 tablespoons per serving)*

| | |
|---|---|
| 6 | tablespoons vegetable oil |
| 2 | teaspoons chopped fresh parsley |
| 2 | teaspoons chopped fresh chives |
| 2 | tablespoons chopped fresh chervil or 2 teaspoon dried chervil |
| | Black pepper to taste |
| 1/2 | cup rice vinegar |
| 2 | tablespoons water |
| 3 | cloves garlic, minced |
| 2 | teaspoons dried mustard |

In a blender, combine all of the ingredients, and blend thoroughly.

*Exchanges per Serving:*
Fats: 2 1/4

*Nutritional Information per Serving:*
Calories: 64
Carbohydrate: 7%
Protein: 1%
Fat: 92%
Fiber: trace
Calcium: 7 mg

••••

# ••••*Lemon-Tarragon Dressing*

*Makes 4 Servings (2 tablespoons per serving)*

| | |
|---|---|
| 1/4 | cup fresh lemon juice |
| 2 | tablespoons water |
| 1 | teaspoon dijon mustard (prepared) |
| | Cayenne pepper to taste |
| 2 | tablespoons vegetable oil |
| 1 1/2 | teaspoons chopped fresh tarragon or 1/2 teaspoon dried tarragon |

In a blender, combine the lemon juice, water, mustard, and pepper; and blend thoroughly. Add the oil and tarragon, and blend well.

**Exchanges per Serving:**
Fats: 1 1/2

**Nutritional Information per Serving:**
Calories: 44
Carbohydrate: 9%
Protein: 1%
Fat: 90%
Fiber: trace
Calcium: 3 mg

♦ ♦ ♦ ♦

# ···· *Oregano Dressing*

*Makes 4 Servings (2 tablespoons per serving)*

3   tablespoons red wine vinegar or rice vinegar
1   tablespoon water
1   tablespoon fresh lemon juice
3   tablespoons virgin olive oil
2   tablespoons minced fresh parsley
1   tablespoon chopped fresh oregano or 3/4 teaspoon dried
     oregano
     Black pepper to taste

In a blender, combine all of the ingredients, and blend
thoroughly.

*Exchanges per Serving:*
Fats: 2 1/4

*Nutritional Information per Serving:*
Calories: 122
Carbohydrate: 6%
Protein: 1%
Fat: 93%
Fiber: trace
Calcium: 12 mg

◆ ◆ ◆ ◆

# ••••*Sesame Orange Dressing*

*Makes 4 Servings (2 tablespoons per serving)*

3/4   **cup orange juice (2 oranges juiced)**
1/4   **cup sesame oil**
  3   **tablespoons sesame seeds**

Combine all of the ingredients in a mixing bowl. Mix well with a fork, and serve over salads.

**Exchanges per Serving:**
Fruits: 1/4
Fats: 3

**Nutritional Information per Serving:**
Calories: 196
Carbohydrate: 16%
Protein: 11%
Fat: 73%
Fiber: 3 g
Calcium: 18 mg

••••

# •••• *Sunflower Salad Dressing*

*Makes 4 Servings (2 tablespoons per serving)*

| | |
|---|---|
| 1 | cup hulled sunflower seeds |
| 1/2 | cup sunflower oil |
| 1/4 | cup lemon juice |
| 1/2 | cup soft tofu |
| 1 | tablespoon tamari soy sauce |
| 1/2 | tablespoon water |
| 1/2 | teaspoon basil |
| 1/2 | teaspoon thyme |

Combine all of the ingredients in a blender or food processor, and blend for 1 minute or until creamy.

*Exchanges per Serving:*
Legumes: 1/4
Fats: 6 1/2

*Nutritional Information per Serving:*
Calories: 212
Carbohydrate: 5%
Protein: 4%
Fat: 91%
Fiber: 4.6 g
Calcium: 14 mg

◆◆◆◆

# •••• *Tomato Salad Dressing*

*Makes 4 Servings (2 tablespoons per serving)*

| | |
|---|---|
| 1/2 | cup tomato juice |
| 1/2 | cup extra virgin olive oil* |
| 3 | tablespoons lemon juice |
| 1/2 | teaspoon basil leaves |
| 1/4 | teaspoon oregano leaves |
| 1 | clove garlic, crushed |

Combine all of the ingredients in a food processor, and blend for 2 minutes.

**Exchanges per Serving:**
Vegetables: 1/4
Fats: 6

**Nutritional Information per Serving:**
Calories: 259
Carbohydrate: 3%
Protein: 0%
Fat: 97%
Fiber: 0.85 g
Calcium: 11 mg

*Safflower oil or sunflower oil can be substituted for olive oil.

••••

# ••••*Vinaigrette Dressing*

*Makes 6 Servings (1 tablespoon per serving)*

1    tablespoon wine vinegar
4    tablespoons olive oil
1    tablespoon chopped herbs (parsley or oregano)
     Lite Salt or salt substitute
     Freshly ground black pepper

Mix together the vinegar and 3 tablespoons of the oil. Add the salt, pepper, and herbs, and mix again. Taste the dressing; if it's too vinegary, add the remaining oil until you get the flavor just right. Pour the dressing into a small jug or bowl, and blend it again just before you serve it. A small wire whisk is particularly handy to ensure the complete blending of oil and vinegar, which separate so easily. This dressing is also nice with the addition of a tablespoon of chopped herbs or a little mustard, depending on what you're going to serve it with; a dollop of brown mustard will make the consistency creamy and smooth.

*Exchanges per Serving:*
Fats: 1 1/2

*Nutritional Information per Serving:*
Calories: 64
Carbohydrate: 3%
Protein: 0%
Fat: 97%
Fiber: 0 g
Calcium: 5 mg

◆ ◆ ◆ ◆

## ◆ Salads ◆

These salads offer incredible variety, yet each can be combined with a number of different cuisines. As salads must become a big part of your diet, you should mix things up and continually try new tastes.

# ••••*Chinese Bean Salad*

*Makes 4 Servings*

| | |
|---|---|
| 1 | pound green beans, trimmed and cut into 2-inch-long julienne strips |
| 1 | tablespoon finely minced ginger |
| 1 | teaspoon finely minced garlic |
| 1 | tablespoon rice vinegar |
| 1 | teaspoon oriental sesame oil |
| 2 | teaspoons low-sodium soy sauce |
| 1/4 | teaspoon ground black or white pepper |
| 2 | tablespoons lightly toasted sesame seeds |

Steam the green beans in a basket for approximately 5 minutes, until tender-crisp. Cool them immediately under cold water to stop the cooking. Transfer to a serving bowl, and set aside. In a small bowl, combine the ginger, garlic, safflower oil, vinegar, sesame oil, soy sauce, and pepper. Pour this over the green beans, and toss to coat well. Chill for 1 hour or more. Stir in the sesame seeds just before serving.

**Exchanges per Serving:**
Vegetables: 1
Fats: 3/4

*Nutritional Information per Serving:*
Calories: 83
Carbohydrate: 53%
Protein: 20%
Fat: 27%
Fiber: 1.5 g
Calcium: 61 mg

*Comments:* If necessary, regular vinegar can substitute for the rice vinegar. Sprouted beans (mung, kidney, soy, garbanzo, etc.) can also be added.

◆◆◆◆

# ••••*Curried Coleslaw*

*Makes 4 Servings*

2    cups finely chopped cabbage
1    cup finely chopped carrot, apple, and lemon (or pulp from juice extractor)
1    cup raisins
1    tablespoon curry powder
2    tablespoons fat-free mayonnaise
2    tablespoons nonfat yogurt
1    apple, finely chopped

Combine all of the ingredients in a bowl, and stir to coat. Cover and refrigerate for 4 hours before serving.

*Exchanges per Serving:*
Vegetables: 1               Fruits: 1 1/4          Milk: 1/4

*Nutritional Information per Serving:*
Calories: 128          Protein: 4%          Fiber: 6 g
Carbohydrate: 82%          Fat: 14%          Calcium: 38 mg

*Comments:* This is a much more healthful alternative to store-bought coleslaws; and it tastes better, too.

◆ ◆ ◆ ◆

# ••••*Fruit Salad with Maple Dressing*

*Makes 4 Servings*

1    fresh pineapple, diced in 1-inch chunks
2    golden delicious apples, pared, cored, and sliced
1    ripe pear, pared, cored, and sliced
1    banana, sliced
1    cup fresh strawberries, sliced
1/4  cup maple syrup
1/4  cup apple juice
1/4  cup chopped pitted dates (optional)
1/4  cup golden raisins (optional)
     Romaine lettuce leaves

Combine the pineapple, apples, pear, banana, and strawberries in a bowl. In another bowl, mix the maple syrup, apple juice, and dates and raisins (if used). Mix the maple syrup mixture into the apple mixture. Toss lightly to moisten all of the fruit pieces. Cover and let stand for 30 minutes in the refrigerator. When ready to serve, line a salad bowl with the lettuce leaves, and arrange the salad in the bowl.

*Exchanges per Serving:*
Vegetables: 1/2
Fruits: 3

*Nutritional Information per Serving:*

| | |
|---|---|
| Calories: 244 | Fat: 3% |
| Carbohydrate: 94% | Fiber: 8 g |
| Protein: 3% | Calcium: 38 mg |

*Comments:* You can substitute fresh peaches, melon, cherries, or other fruit of the season for the pears and apples.

◆◆◆◆

# ◆◆◆◆ *Hearty Vegetable Salad*

*Makes 6 Servings*

|  |  |
|---|---|
| 1 | tablespoon olive oil |
| 1/2 | cup red wine vinegar |
| 1/3 | cup chopped fresh parsley |
| 2 | tablespoons fresh lemon juice |
| 1 | clove garlic, minced |
| 2 | teaspoons dried basil, crumbled |
| 3/4 | teaspoon Lite Salt or salt substitute |
| 1/4 | teaspoon freshly ground pepper |
| 3 | large boiling potatoes, peeled, cooked, and thinly sliced |
| 1 1/2 | pounds baby carrots, cooked |
| 1 1/2 | pounds green beans, cooked and cut to same length as carrots |
| 3 | beets, cooked and thinly sliced |
|  | Lettuce leaves |

Mix together the oils, vinegar, parsley, lemon juice, garlic, basil, salt, and pepper. Place the potato, carrot, and beans in one bowl; and place the beet in a smaller bowl. Pour vinaigrette over the vegetables, and stir gently. Cover and marinate for 3 hours at room temperature, or refrigerate overnight. To serve, line a platter with lettuce leaves, and arrange the vegetables over top.

*Exchanges per Serving:*
Vegetables: 3
Grains and starches: 1 1/2
Fats: 1/2

*Nutritional Information per Serving:*
Calories: 279
Protein: 8%
Carbohydrate: 68%
Fat: 24%
Fiber: 3.6 g
Calcium: 62.7 mg

*Comments:* This great-tasting salad can be used as a main dish for someone on a weight-loss program. It is very filling and quite satisfying, yet low in calories.

◆◆◆◆

# ••••*Insalata Mista*

*Makes 4 Servings*

| | |
|---|---|
| 1 | head lettuce |
| 1 | fennel bulb |
| 1/2 | small cucumber, sliced |
| 6 | radishes, trimmed and sliced |
| 1 | celery heart, chopped |
| 1 | small green pepper, cored, seeded, and sliced |
| 4 | scallions, thinly sliced |
| 2 | ripe, firm tomatoes |
| | Lite Salt or salt substitute |
| 2 | tablespoons olive oil |
| 2 | teaspoons cider vinegar or lemon juice |

Pull off and discard any bruised or blemished outer leaves of the lettuce. Wash the remaining lettuce, and shake dry in a salad basket; then tear the leaves into bite-sized pieces, and place in a salad bowl. Trim the stalks, base, and coarse outer leaves from the fennel; cut downward into thin slices; and then cut into strips. Add these to the salad bowl with the cucumber, radishes, celery, pepper, and scallions. Cut the tomatoes into quarters and then into eighths, and add to the bowl. When ready to serve, sprinkle the salad with a little salt, add the oil and the cider vinegar or lemon juice, and toss lightly together. Serve immediately.

*Exchanges per Serving:*
Vegetables: 3/4                     Fats: 1/2

*Nutritional Information per Serving:*
Calories: 70             Protein: 19%        Fiber: 5 g
Carbohydrate: 52%        Fat: 30%            Calcium: 50 mg

*Comments:* This is the ideal salad to accompany pasta or pizza.

••••

# ••••*Jicama Salad*

*Makes 12 Servings*

| | |
|---|---|
| 1 | large jicama, peeled and julienned |
| 2 | cups Jerusalem artichokes, julienned |
| 1 | bunch watercress, shopped coarsely |
| 4 | green onions, finely diced |
| 1 | medium red bell pepper, julienned |
| 1 | clove garlic, diced |
| 1 | tablespoon vegetable oil |
| 1/4 | cup cider vinegar |
| 1/4 | cup spicy mustard |
| 1 | teaspoon snipped fresh dill, diced |
| 2 | sprigs snipped fresh parsley, diced |
| 2 | sprigs cilantro, diced |
| | Black pepper to taste |

In a large bowl, combine all of the ingredients, and mix well. Cover tightly, and marinate for 1 hour. Toss again before serving.

*Exchanges per Serving:*
Vegetables: 2
Fats: 1/4

*Nutritional Information per Serving:*

| | | |
|---|---|---|
| Calories: 105 | Protein: 10% | Fiber: 1 g |
| Carbohydrate: 62% | Fat: 28% | Calcium: 23 mg |

*Comments:* This salad makes good use of several vegetables that are beneficial to diabetics.

••••

# ••••*Lentil Salad*

*Makes 4 Servings*

| | |
|---|---|
| 1 | cup dried lentils |
| 2 | quarts water |
| 1 | bay leaf |
| 1 | clove garlic, whole, peeled |
| 1 | teaspoon salt |
| 1/4 | cup scallions |
| 1/2 | cup chopped fresh parsley |
| 1 | teaspoon prepared mustard |
| 1/2 | teaspoon black pepper |
| 1 | tablespoon olive oil |
| 1 | tablespoon lemon juice |
| 1/2 | cup grated carrots |

Clean the lentils and put them into a large pot with the water, bay leaf, garlic, and salt. Heat to boiling. Turn the heat off, and let stand for 30 minutes. Drain. Turn into a mixing bowl. Add the onion, parsley, mustard, black pepper, oil, and lemon juice; and blend thoroughly. Garnish with grated carrots.

**Exchanges per Serving:**

| Vegetables: 1/2 | Legumes: 1 | Fats: 1 |
|---|---|---|

**Nutritional Information per Serving:**

| Calories: 160 | Protein: 18% | Fiber: 2 g |
|---|---|---|
| Carbohydrate: 65% | Fat: 17% | Calcium: 35 mg |

*Comments:* This highly nutritious salad is great for lunch, especially for diabetics.

••••

# •••• *Mediterranean Salad*

*Makes 4 Servings*

| | |
|---|---|
| 1 | cucumber, sliced |
| 1 | bunch radishes, trimmed |
| 1 | red bell pepper, cut into strips |
| 1 | green bell pepper, cut into strips |
| 3 | tomatoes, cut into wedges |
| 1/2 | bunch chicory or curly endive lettuce, shredded |
| 6 | scallions, sliced |
| 3 | tablespoons Oregano Dressing (see Salad Dressings) |
| 2 | tablespoons crumbled feta cheese |

In a medium bowl, combine the cucumber, radishes, peppers, tomatoes, chicory (or lettuce), and onions. Add the Oregano Dressing, and toss to coat well. Sprinkle with feta cheese.

*Exchanges per Serving*
Vegetables: 1
Fats: 1/2
Meat: 1/2

*Nutritional Information per Serving:*
Calories: 125
Carbohydrate: 58%
Protein: 12%
Fat: 30%
Fiber: 2 g
Calcium: 135 mg

*Comments:* This salad goes extremely well with pasta, pizza, and other Mediterranean foods.

••••

# ••••*Orange and Fennel Salad*

*Makes 4 Servings*

| | |
|---|---|
| 2 | large or 4 small fennel bulbs |
| 4 | oranges |
| 1 | medium lemon |
| 1 | tablespoon olive oil |
| | Lite Salt or salt substitute |
| | Freshly ground black pepper |
| 8 | black olives |

Wash, trim, and cut the fennel lengthwise into thick wedges. Cut the tops and bottoms off the oranges. Hold them over a serving dish, and cut away the peel and white pith with a small sharp or serrated knife. Slice thinly across the segments, and arrange the slices in a shallow serving dish with the fennel. Cut off the peel and pith from half of the lemon, and chop the flesh. Sprinkle over the orange and fennel. Over the top, pour the olive oil and a little lemon juice from the remaining half lemon. Season with a little salt and a few twists of freshly ground black pepper. Toss well. Cover and chill until required. Just before serving, decorate with black olives.

*Exchanges per Serving:*
Vegetables: 1          Fruits: 1          Fats: 1

*Nutritional Information per Serving:*
Calories: 170          Protein: 12%          Fiber: 3.5 g
Carbohydrate: 58%          Fat: 30%          Calcium: 100 mg

*Comments:* This salad offers some unique healing features, due to the combination of the flavonoids in the orange and the healing compounds (coumarins) in the fennel.

••••

# ••••*Rice, Bean, and Corn Salad*

*Makes 4 Servings*

| | |
|---|---|
| 2 | cups cooked brown rice |
| | 16-ounce can or 2 cups cooked red kidney beans, rinsed and drained |
| 1 1/2 | cup frozen corn |
| 4 | scallions, chopped |
| 1/8 | cup olive oil |
| 1/8 | cup fresh lime juice |
| 1/8 | cup cider vinegar |
| 1 | tablespoon brown sugar |
| 2 | fresh or pickled jalapeños, minced |
| 1 | teaspoon chili powder |
| 1/2 | teaspoon cumin |
| 1/2 | teaspoon salt |

Mix together, and serve with lime wedges.

*Exchanges per Serving:*
Vegetables: 1/4
Fruits: 1/4
Grains and starches: 2
Legumes: 1
Fats: 1/2

*Nutritional Information per Serving:*

| | | |
|---|---|---|
| Calories: 303 | Protein: 11% | Fiber: 11 g |
| Carbohydrate: 61% | Fat: 28% | Calcium: 64 mg |

*Comments:* This extremely nutritious and hearty salad can be used as an entrée, especially during the hot summer months.

••••

# ••••*Vegetable Rice Salad*

*Makes 6 Servings*

*Salad*

| | |
|---|---|
| 2 | cups cooked long-grain brown rice |
| 1/4 | cup finely sliced radish (about 3 large) |
| 1/2 | cup peeled, seeded, and finely diced cucumber |
| 1/2 | cup finely diced red bell pepper |
| 1/4 | cup finely diced celery |
| 1/4 | cup thinly sliced scallion |

*Dressing*

| | |
|---|---|
| 2 | tablespoons olive oil |
| 1/4 | cup freshly grated Parmesan cheese |
| 3 | tablespoons cider vinegar |
| 2 | tablespoons plain yogurt |
| 1 | tablespoon minced fresh basil (or other fresh herb) |
| 1/2 | teaspoon prepared mustard |
| 1/2 | teaspoon Lite Salt or salt substitute |
| 1/4 | teaspoon freshly ground pepper |

*Garnish*

| | |
|---|---|
| | Lettuce leaves |
| | Tomato wedges |
| 2 | tablespoons pumpkin seeds (optional) |

*For salad:* Combine all of the ingredients in a large bowl. Taste and adjust seasoning.

*For dressing:* Blend all of the ingredients in a medium-size mixing bowl. Add the dressing to the salad, mixing well. Taste and adjust seasoning. Cover tightly, and refrigerate overnight.

*To serve:* Bring the salad to room temperature. Arrange the lettuce leaves on a large serving platter. Toss the salad lightly, and mound it in the center. Garnish with tomato wedges. Sprinkle with pumpkin seeds if desired.

*Exchanges per Serving:*
Vegetables: 1/2  Grains and starches: 2/3     Fats: 1

*Nutritional Information per Serving:*
Calories: 115          Protein: 12%        Fiber: 1.6 g
Carbohydrate: 61%      Fat: 27%            Calcium: 179 mg

**Comments:** This delicious and spicy salad works very well with Indian and East Asian dishes.

◆◆◆◆

## ◆◆◆◆ *Waldorf Salad*

*Makes 6 Servings*

*Dressing*

| | |
|---|---|
| 10 | ounces firm tofu |
| 1/2 | cup nonfat yogurt |
| 3 | tablespoons honey |
| 2 | tablespoons fresh lemon juice |
| | Juice of 1 orange |
| 1/2 | teaspoon ground cloves, cinnamon, nutmeg, or cardamom |
| 1/4 | teaspoon vanilla extract (optional) |

*Salad*

| | |
|---|---|
| 2 | apples, chopped |
| 2 | pears, chopped |
| 4 | celery ribs, chopped |
| 1/2 | cup raisins |
| 1 | cup walnuts, chopped |

*For dressing:* Process all of the ingredients in a blender or food processor until smooth and creamy. This dressing can be refrigerated for up to a week. The recipe makes about 2 cups of dressing.

*For salad:* Mix the ingredients together with the dressing, and serve chilled.

**Exchanges per Serving:**
Vegetables: 1/3
Fruits: 1 1/2
Legumes: 1/3
Fats: 1
Milk: 1/4

**Nutritional Information per Serving:**
Calories: 235
Carbohydrates: 53%
Protein: 22%
Fat: 25%
Fiber: 4.8 g
Calcium: 203 mg

**Comments:** This is a fantastic salad, from both taste and nutritional perspectives.

◆◆◆

# ···· *Zucchini and Caper Salad*

*Makes 4 Servings*

*Salad*

4   large zucchini, trimmed (quarter zucchini lengthwise; then cut into 1/2-inch slices)
1   small red bell pepper, seeded and finely chopped
2   tablespoons drained capers
1   tablespoon chopped fresh parsley
1   head red-leaf lettuce, leaves separated

*Dressing*

1   tablespoon virgin olive oil
1   tablespoon fresh lemon juice
1/2   teaspoon dry mustard
1/4   teaspoon black pepper

In a medium-size bowl, combine the zucchini, red pepper, capers, and parsley; and Mix together. In a small bowl, combine the dressing ingredients, and mix thoroughly. Pour the dressing over the zucchini mixture, and toss to coat well. Pile the zucchini mixture in the centers of four individual lettuce-lined serving bowls, just before the salads are to be served.

**Exchanges per Serving:**
Vegetables: 3/4                    Fats: 3/4

**Nutritional Information per Serving:**
Calories: 120              Protein: 16%          Fiber: 1 g
Carbohydrate: 54%          Fat: 30%              Calcium: 33 mg

**Comments:** This is a great summer salad for using the abundance of fresh zucchini produced in a home garden.

◆ ◆ ◆ ◆

# 5

## ••••Breads and Muffins

Whole grains and other sources of complex carbohydrates should serve as the foundation of a healthy diet. The whole-grain recipes provided in this chapter offer considerable nutritional advantages over their store-bought counterparts. And you'll enjoy preparing these easy, straightforward recipes as well as eating them. They are delicious.

## ••••Basic Whole Wheat Bread

*Makes 22 to 24 Servings (two loaves; one slice per serving)*

|       |                                               |
| ----- | --------------------------------------------- |
| 2     | envelopes active dry yeast                    |
| 3 1/2 | cups very warm water                          |
| 2     | tablespoons honey                             |
| 1     | teaspoon olive oil                            |
|       | Enough dry nonfat milk powder to make 1 quart of milk |
| 1/2   | cup soy flour                                 |
| 1     | tablespoon salt                               |
| 9     | cups whole wheat flour (approximately)        |

In a large mixing bowl, soften the yeast in warm water. Stir in the honey, and set aside for 5 to 10 minutes. Stir in the oil, milk powder, soy flour, and salt. Add enough whole wheat flour to make a stiff dough. Knead the dough in the bowl for about 5 to 10 minutes, or until smooth. Cover the bowl with a clean cloth, and let the dough rise until it has doubled in bulk (about 1 hour).

Punch the dough down, and then knead it for 1 to 2 minutes. Divide the dough in half, and shape it into loaves. Place each half in a greased loaf pan (9 × 5 × 3 inches), cover, and let it rise until it has again doubled in size (about 35 minutes). Bake at 350°F for 30 to 35 minutes or until done. The bread should sound hollow when tapped. Cool on a wire rack.

*Exchanges per Serving:*
Fruits: 1/8
Grains and starches: 2 1/2
Fats: 1/8
Milk: 1/8

*Nutritional Information per Serving:*
Calories: 172
Carbohydrate: 79%
Protein: 12%
Fat: 9%
Fiber: 5 g
Calcium: 37 mg

*Comments:* The soy flour nutritionally fortifies this recipe by improving its amino acid profile.

◆◆◆◆

# ••••*Apple Carrot Muffins*

*Makes 12 Servings (one muffin per serving)*

| | |
|---|---|
| 2 1/2 | cups whole wheat flour |
| 1/2 | cup soy powder |
| 1 | teaspoon baking soda |
| 1/4 | teaspoon salt |
| 1/4 | teaspoon nutmeg |
| 1/4 | teaspoon cinnamon |
| 1/8 | cup oil |
| 3/4 | cup honey |
| 1 | teaspoon vanilla extract |
| 1/2 | cup apple, grated |
| 1/2 | cup carrot, grated |

Preheat oven to 400°F. In a medium-size bowl, combine all the dry ingredients. Combine all the liquid ingredients in a large bowl; stir in the apple and carrot. Add the dry ingredients to the liquid mixture. Oil one muffin tin; then spoon the batter into the cups until each cup is two-thirds full. Bake for 20 minutes, or until a toothpick stuck in the center of the muffin comes out clean.

*Exchanges per Serving:*
Fruits: 1      Grains and starches: 2      Fats: 1/8

*Nutritional Information per Serving:*
Calories: 220            Protein: 15%         Fiber: 4 g
Carbohydrate: 60%       Fat: 25%             Calcium: 53 mg

*Comments:* This is a great way to start the day, along with a glass of fresh orange juice.

◆ ◆ ◆ ◆

# ····*Bagels*

*Makes 24 Servings (one bagel per serving)*

| | |
|---|---|
| 2 | tablespoons bakers' yeast |
| 5 | tablespoons date sugar |
| 2 | cups warm water |
| 2 | cups whole wheat pastry flour |
| 1/8 | cup oil |
| 1/2 | teaspoon salt |
| 4 | cups whole wheat pastry flour (additional) |
| 3 | quarts of water |

In a large bowl, combine the yeast, date sugar, and warm water. Slowly add 2 cups of flour. Mix well and let rise for 10 minutes. Beat in the oil, salt, and about 4 more cups flour. Mix well. Turn the dough onto a floured board, and knead for 10 minutes. The dough should be soft but not sticky. Place the dough in an oiled bowl; cover with a clean dishcloth, and allow to rise for 45 minutes. Turn onto a floured board, and knead for 10 minutes more. Cut pieces of dough, and roll into ropes approximately 7 inches long and 1 inch around. Join the ends to form a doughnut shape. Let rise for 5 minutes.

Preheat oven to 375°F. Bring the 3 quarts of water to a boil in a large soup pot. Drop four or five of the rings, one at a time (risen side down), into the boiling water, and put the lid on. Boil for 30 seconds on one side, and then for 30 seconds on the other, maintaining a rapid boil the entire time. Remove the bagels with a slotted spatula, and place them about 1/2 inch apart on a well-oiled cookie sheet. Bake for 25 to 30 minutes or until golden brown.

**Exchanges per Serving:**
Fruits: 1/4    Grains and starches: 1        Fats: 1/8

*Nutritional Information per Serving:*
Calories: 98
Carbohydrate: 77%
Protein: 12%
Fat: 11%
Fiber: 3 g
Calcium: 32 mg

*Comments:* Raisins and other dried fruit can be added to the recipe if desired.

◆◆◆◆

# ••••*Banana-Oatmeal Pecan Bread*

*Makes 8 Servings (one loaf)*

| | |
|---|---|
| 1/4 | cup vegetable oil |
| 1/8 | cup honey |
| 2 | egg whites |
| 3 | bananas, mashed |
| 1/4 | cup nonfat vanilla yogurt |
| 1/2 | teaspoon vanilla extract |
| 1 | teaspoon baking powder |
| 1 | teaspoon baking soda |
| 1/2 | cup rolled oats |
| 2 | cups whole wheat flour |
| 3/4 | cup pecans |

Preheat oven to 350°F. In a medium-size bowl, stir together the vegetable oil and honey until the mixture has an even consistency. Stir in the egg whites, one at a time. Stir in the bananas, yogurt, and vanilla. When these are well-blended, mix in the baking powder, baking soda, and salt; then blend in the oats, flour, and pecans until all of the ingredients are well-combined. Turn the mixture into an oiled loaf pan (9 × 5 × 3 inches). Bake at 350°F for 55 minutes or until a toothpick inserted in the center comes out clean. Remove the loaf from the pan, and cool on a wire rack. Serve warm or cooled. This bread is slightly sweet and is good served with fresh fruit for breakfast.

*Exchanges per Serving:*
Grains and Starches: 1
Fats: 1
Milk: 1/8

*Nutritional Information per Serving:*
Calories: 112
Carbohydrate: 67%
Protein: 10%
Fat: 23%
Fiber: 7 g
Calcium: 9 mg

*Comments:* This bread is extremely rich in potassium and other nutritional factors necessary for proper heart function.

◆◆◆◆

# •••• *Bran Muffins*

*Makes 12 Servings (one muffin per serving)*

|       |                        |
|-------|------------------------|
| 1 1/4 | cups whole wheat flour |
| 1     | cup bran               |
| 1     | teaspoon baking soda   |
| 1     | teaspoon cinnamon      |
| 1/8   | cup oil                |
| 1/3 to 1/2 | cup honey         |
| 1     | cup nonfat milk        |
| 1/2   | teaspoon vanilla extract |

Preheat oven to 400°F. Combine all of the dry ingredients in a large bowl. Mix all of the liquid ingredients in a large bowl; add the dry ingredients, and mix well. Oil one muffin tin, and sprinkle each cup with flour. Spoon batter into each cup until it is half full. Bake for 25 minutes.

*Exchanges per Serving:*
Fruits: 1/2
Grains and starches: 1
Fats: 1/3
Milk: 1/12

*Nutritional Information per Serving:*
Calories: 114
Carbohydrate: 70%
Protein: 10%

Fat: 20%
Fiber: 3 g
Calcium: 34 mg

*Comments:* Oat bran can substitute for wheat bran in this recipe.

◆ ◆ ◆

# •••• *Dark Peasant Bread*

*Makes 8 Servings (one loaf)*

| | |
|---|---|
| 1 1/2 | cups very warm water |
| 1 1/2 | tablespoons dry yeast |
| 1/4 | cup molasses |
| 1 | cup rye flour |
| 2 | teaspoons caraway seeds |
| 1/4 | cup carob powder, sifted |
| 4 to 4 1/2 | cups whole wheat flour |

Combine and dissolve the first three ingredients, and let sit until bubbly (about 10 minutes). Beat in well 2 cups of whole wheat flour. Place in a warm area until double in bulk (about 20 minutes). Stir in the next five ingredients. Then add, 1/2 cup at a time, enough whole wheat flour to make a soft dough that can be kneaded. Knead well, for about 5 minutes. Place in a clean, oiled bowl, and cover with towel. Let rise until again double (about 30 to 40 minutes). Punch down and knead. Shape into a loaf, and place in a lecithin-oiled pan. Let rise again until double. Preheat oven to 350° and bake for 40 to 45 minutes. Makes 8 servings (one loaf).

*Exchanges per Serving:*
Grains and starches: 3

*Nutritional Information per Serving:*

| | | |
|---|---|---|
| Calories: 210 | Protein: 12% | Fiber: 7 g |
| Carbohydrate: 85% | Fat: 3% | Calcium: 49 mg |

*Comments:* This interesting bread is certainly worth a try, especially if you like rye.

•••

# •••• Four-grain Bread

*Makes 24 Servings (two loaves; one slice per serving)*

| | |
|---|---|
| 1 | cup sprouted bulgur wheat |
| 2 | cups warm water |
| 1/2 | cup honey |
| 2 | packages dry active yeast |
| 2 | tablespoons vegetable oil |
| 6 | cups whole wheat flour |
| 1 | tablespoon salt |
| 1/2 | cup cornmeal |
| 1 | cup rolled oats |

Make sure that all of the ingredients are at room temperature. Put the bulgur in a small bowl, cover it with boiling water, and let it soak for 30 minutes. Put the 2 cups of warm water in a large bowl, and stir in the honey and yeast. Let sit for 5 minutes or so, or until bubbles form on the surface of the mixture. Add the oil, 5 cups of the whole-wheat flour, and salt. Beat vigorously with a wooden spoon, 100 strokes. In two batches, put the bulgur into a strainer, and press out all the liquid. Then add the bulgur to the dough, along with the cornmeal, the rolled oats, and the remaining cup of whole wheat flour. Beat in these ingredients until they are well-mixed. The dough will become difficult to handle. Turn the dough onto a floured board or work surface, and knead diligently for 10 minutes. Keep flouring the work surface as the dough becomes too sticky to handle.

Place the dough in a greased bowl, pat it down, and then turn it greased side up. Cover the top of the bowl with a newspaper, and allow the dough to rise in a warm place until it doubles in size. When it has doubled, punch down the dough to its original size, cover it with the newspaper, and let it rise again. When the dough doubles again, punch it down, and divide it into two equal-size portions. Grease two 1 1/2–quart bread pans, shape the dough into two loaves, and place these in the pans. Allow the dough to rise in the pans until it reaches the top of the pans.

Preheat oven to 350°. Brush the top of each loaf with a light coating of oil. After 25 minutes, brush the top of each loaf with oil again. Bake for 50 minutes or until the loaves are nicely browned. Remove the loaves from the pans, brush again with a light coating of oil, and cool on a wire rack.

*Exchanges per Serving:*
Fruits: 1/3
Grains and starches: 2
Fats: 1/4

*Nutritional Information per Serving:*
Calories: 175
Carbohydrate: 77%
Protein: 13%
Fat: 10%
Fiber: 4 g
Calcium: 19 mg

*Comments:* To freeze a loaf, allow it to cool thoroughly; then wrap it in aluminum foil, and place this in a plastic bag.

◆◆◆◆

# •••• *French Bread*

*Makes 22 to 24 Servings (two loaves; one slice per serving)*

*Bread*

| | |
|---|---|
| 2 | tablespoons yeast |
| 1/2 | cup lukewarm water |
| 1 | teaspoon blackstrap molasses |
| 3/4 | cup lukewarm water, potato water, or vegetable water |
| 1 1/2 | teaspoons salt |
| 1 | teaspoon honey |
| 3 | cups whole wheat flour |
| 1 | teaspoon olive oil |

*Glaze*

| | |
|---|---|
| 1 | teaspoon cornstarch |
| 1 | teaspoon cold water |
| 1/2 | cup boiling water |

Sprinkle the yeast on top of a mixture of 1/2 cup of the water and the molasses. Set aside for 10 minutes in a warm, draft-free place. Beat together 3/4 cup of lukewarm water, the salt, the honey, the flour, and the oil. Add the yeast to this mix. Stir until well-mixed. Turn the dough onto a lightly floured board. Knead. Place the dough in an oiled bowl, brush lightly with olive oil, and cover with a clean towel. Let the dough rise in a warm place until it has doubled in bulk (about 40 minutes). Punch it down and let it rise again until it has al-most doubled in bulk (about 30 minutes). To make the glaze, combine cornstarch and cold water; gradually add boiling wa-ter; cook until smooth; and then allow to cool slightly. When the bread dough has risen, divide it into two equal portions. Press each piece of dough into an oblong, about 15 inches by 10 inches. Beginning with the wide side, roll the dough up lightly. Seal the edges by pinching them together. With hands at each end, roll the dough gently back and forth to lengthen the loaf and to taper the ends.

Place the loaves on a greased baking sheet, and brush them with cornstarch glaze. Let rise, uncovered, for about 1 1/2 hours. Brush again with cornstarch glaze. Make 1/4-inch slashes in the top of the dough at 2-inch intervals. Bake at 400°F for 10 minutes. Remove from oven, and brush again with cornstarch glaze. Return to oven, and bake for 20 minutes or until golden brown. Because of its shape, this bread is best eaten right away; it tends to dry out quickly.

*Exchanges per Serving:*
Fruits: 1/8
Grains and starches: 1
Fats: 1/8

*Nutritional Information per Serving:*
Calories: 66
Carbohydrate: 82%
Protein: 11%
Fat: 7%
Fiber: 2 g
Calcium: 9 mg

*Comments:* For a crustier French loaf, place a pan of boiling water in the bottom of the oven during baking.

◆◆◆◆

# •••• Nut Loaf

*Makes 4 Servings*

| | |
|---|---|
| 1 | cup chopped cooked carrots |
| 1/2 | cup chopped walnuts |
| 1 | cup bread crumbs |
| 1 | small onion, chopped |
| 2 | egg whites |
| 1/2 | stalk celery, chopped |
| | 8-ounce can tomato sauce |
| 1/2 | teaspoon olive oil |

Preheat oven to 350°F. Mix all of the ingredients except the tomato sauce. Spoon into an oiled pan. Bake for 30 minutes. Five minutes before removing from oven, cover with tomato sauce.

*Exchanges per Serving:*
Vegetables: 1/4
Grains and starches: 1 1/4
Fats: 1 1/2

*Nutritional Information per Serving:*
Calories: 136
Carbohydrate: 56%
Protein: 14%
Fat: 30%
Fiber: 5 g
Calcium: 25 mg

*Comments:* This highly nutritious bread is rich in protein and potassium.

•••

# ····*Nutritional Yeast Pancakes*

*Makes 4 Servings*

| | |
|---|---|
| 1/2 | cup nutritional yeast |
| 3/4 | cup whole wheat flour |
| 3/4 | cup water |
| 1 | teaspoon vegetable oil |

Combine the yeast, flour, and water in a medium-size bowl, to form a loose flakey mixture. Heat the oil in a large skillet over medium-high heat. Pour the batter into the skillet, forming small circles. Cook for approximately 3 minutes on each side, until the pancakes golden brown and crispy.

*Exchanges per Serving:*
Grains and starches: 2/3
Fats: 1/4

*Nutritional Information per Serving:*
Calories: 65
Carbohydrate: 55%
Protein: 35%
Fat: 10%
Fiber: 0.5 g
Calcium: 16.5 mg

*Comments:* For variety and enhanced nutrition, add small pieces of tofu, strawberries, blueberries, or raisins to the batter before cooking.

◆◆◆◆

# ••••*Oatmeal Scones*

*Makes 8 Servings (one scone per serving)*

| | |
|---|---|
| 1 | cup rolled oats |
| 1/2 | cup plain nonfat yogurt |
| 1/2 | cup whole wheat flour |
| 1/2 | cup unbleached white flour |
| 2 | tablespoons firmly packed light brown sugar |
| 1/2 | teaspoon baking soda |
| | Dash of Lite Salt or salt substitute |
| 3 | tablespoons vegetable oil |
| 1/3 | cup egg substitute |

Preheat oven to 400°F. Grease a baking sheet. Combine the oats and yogurt in a large bowl, and let soak. After 15 minutes, add the egg substitute to this mixture and blend well.

In a separate bowl, mix the flours, sugar, baking powder, baking soda, and salt until well-blended. Using a pastry blender, mix the vegetable oil slowly into the mixture, until the mixture resembles coarse meal. Stir the flour mixture into the oats mixture, and mix these just until evenly moistened; then gather the mixture into a ball. If it is too dry, add a little more yogurt. Turn the mixture onto a lightly floured board and knead 5 times. Form into a circle about 3/4 inch thick; and with a knife that has been dipped in flour, cut the circle into 8 wedges. Place these a few inches apart on the baking sheets, and bake for 15 to 17 minutes. Serve immediately.

*Exchanges per Serving:*
Fruits: 1/4
Grains and starches: 1
Fats: 1 1/4
Milk: 1/8

*Nutritional Information per Serving:*
Calories: 139
Carbohydrates: 64%
Protein: 14%
Fat: 22%
Fiber: 1.1 g
Calcium: 56 mg

*Comments:* Scones are delicious with a little honey spread inside.

◆◆◆◆

# ••••*Old-fashioned Oatmeal Bread*

*Makes 22 to 24 Servings (two loaves; one slice per serving)*

|        |                        |
|-------:|------------------------|
| 2      | envelopes active dry yeast |
| 1/2    | cup warm water         |
| 1/2    | cup molasses           |
| 1/8    | cup vegetable oil      |
| 1 1/4  | cups water             |
| 2      | egg whites             |
| 2      | cups rolled oats       |
| 5 to 5 1/2 | cups whole wheat flour |

Stir the yeast into warm water, and set aside for 5 minutes. Stir again to dissolve. In a large bowl, mix together the molasses, the oil, 1 1/4 cups of water, and the egg whites. Stir in the yeast and then the oats. Add whole wheat flour, using just enough to form a soft dough. You may need to use up to 5 1/2 cups of whole wheat flour. Knead the dough in the bowl for several minutes to develop the gluten. Cover and let rise in a warm, draft-free place for about 1 hour and 15 minutes, or until the dough has doubled in bulk. Punch the dough down, and knead again. Punch the dough down, and knead again. Divide the dough in half, and place it in two oiled loaf pans (9 × 5 × 3 inches). Cover and let rise again until doubled in bulk (about 45 minutes). Bake at 375°F for about 45 minutes or until the loaves sound hollow when tapped. When done, remove from pans and cool on a wire rack.

*Exchanges per Serving:*
Fruits: 1/2
Grains and starches: 2
Fats: 1/3

*Nutritional Information per Serving:*
Calories: 164
Carbohydrate: 76%
Protein: 17%
Fat: 7%
Fiber: 6 g
Calcium: 46 mg

*Comments:* This is a great way to obtain the benefits of oats in your diet.

♦ ♦ ♦ ♦

# •••• *Poppy Seed Bread*

*Makes 22 to 24 Servings (two loaves; one slice per serving)*

| | |
|---|---|
| 1 1/2 | cups rolled oats |
| 1 | cup hot water |
| 1 1/4 | cups warm water |
| 1/4 | cup honey |
| 2 | tablespoons dry yeast |
| 2 | cups whole wheat flour |
| 1/3 | cup olive oil |
| 1/4 | cup sesame seeds |
| 1/4 | cup sunflower seeds |
| 1/4 | cup poppy seeds |
| 1 | teaspoon salt |
| 4 to 5 | cups whole wheat flour |

Place the first two ingredients in a bowl and set it aside. Briskly mix together the next four ingredients, and let sit for 15 minutes. Then stir well together all of the ingredients except the last one. Add the remaining flour, 1 cup at a time, making a soft dough. Place the dough on a floured board or counter. Knead for approximately 5 to 10 minutes. Place in a bowl, covered, in a warm place, and let rise until double (about 30 minutes). Then punch down, knead, and shape into two loaves. Place these into two lecithin-oiled pans. Cover and let rise until almost double (about 20 to 30 minutes). Bake at 350°F for 40 to 45 minutes.

*Exchanges per Serving:*
Fruits: 1/4     Grains and starches: 2          Fats: 1

*Nutritional Information per Serving:*
Calories: 173          Protein: 13%          Fiber: 5 g
Carbohydrate: 63%          Fat: 24%          Calcium: 42 mg

*Comments:* This bread is a rich source of lignans and other fiber components that have been shown to reduce a person's risk for certain cancers, especially colon and breast cancer.

◆◆◆◆

# ◆◆◆◆*Rolls*

*Makes 12 Servings (one roll per serving)*

| | |
|---|---|
| 1 | cup plain nonfat yogurt |
| 1 | teaspoon butter |
| 1/4 | cup water |
| 1 | tablespoon honey |
| 1 | package active dry yeast |
| 1 1/4 | cups white flour |
| 1 1/2 | cups whole wheat flour |
| 1/2 | teaspoon baking soda |
| 1 | egg |
| 1 | teaspoon oregano |
| 1 | teaspoon marjoram |
| 1 | teaspoon basil |
| 2 | tablespoons onion, grated |

In a saucepan, heat together the yogurt, butter, water, and honey until the butter melts. Set this mixture aside, and let it cool to lukewarm. In a large bowl, combine the yeast, 3/4 cup of white flour, 3/4 cup of whole wheat flour, and baking soda. Add the cooled liquid mixture to the yeast–flour mixture; then add egg, spices, and grated onion. Beat at a low speed with an electric mixer for 30 seconds. Beat for 3 minutes at high speed.

Stir in 1/2 cup of white flour and 3/4 cup of whole wheat flour. The dough will still be moist and a little sticky. Place it in a bowl sprayed with vegetable cooking spray, turning it once. Cover the bowl with a towel or plastic wrap. Let it rise until double (about 1 1/2 hours).

Place the dough on a floured board and knead lightly. Divide the dough into 12 even pieces, form these into round balls, and place them into muffin tins sprayed with vegetable cooking spray. Cover, and allow to rise for about 40 minutes. Bake at 400°F for 12 to 15 minutes, or until nicely browned. Remove the rolls from the muffin tins immediately. Serve hot or at room temperature.

*Exchanges per Serving:*
Vegetables: 1/10
Grains and starches: 1 1/2
Fats: 1/3
Milk: 1/5
Meat: 1/12

*Nutritional Information per Serving:*
Calories: 125
Carbohydrate: 77%
Protein: 16%
Fat: 7%
Fiber: 2 g
Calcium: 52 mg

*Comments:* These rolls are absolutely delicious, due largely to the flavor provided by the aromatic herbs.

◆◆◆◆

# •••• Sunflower Power Cookies

*Makes 24 Servings (one cookie per serving)*

| | |
|---|---|
| 1 | cup chopped dried apricots |
| 1 | cup warm water |
| 1/4 | cup raw honey |
| 1 | tablespoon vegetable oil |
| 1 | teaspoon vanilla extract |
| 2 | cups rolled oats |
| 1 | cup whole wheat pastry flour |
| 1/4 | cup toasted wheat germ |
| 1/2 | cup currants or raisins |
| 1 | tablespoon sunflower seeds |
| 2 | tablespoons apple or orange juice, if needed |

Soak the apricots in water for 15 minutes. Whip the next three ingredients together; then combine the next three ingredients, and add them to this wet mixture. Drain the water from the apricots. Fold in the apricots, currants, and sunflower seeds, using apple (or orange) juice to make the batter more pliable if it is too stiff. Press the dough into an oiled baking pan (13 × 9 × 2 inches). Bake at 350°F for 20 to 25 minutes. Cool and cut into squares.

*Exchanges per Serving:*
Fruits: 1      Grains and starches: 1/2      Fats: 1/4

*Nutritional Information per Serving:*
| | | |
|---|---|---|
| Calories: 136 | Protein: 8% | Fiber: 8 g |
| Carbohydrate: 66% | Fat: 26% | Calcium: 75 mg |

*Comments:* Kids love these cookies, and for good reason: they are delicious. They are also far superior nutritionally to store-bought cookies.

•••

# 6

$$\bullet\bullet\bullet\bullet Spreads\ and\ Dips$$

These spreads and dips are fantastic for use when entertaining. You'll find dips that work well with whole-grain corn chips, crackers, and vegetables, along with delicious spreads that can fortify the protein quality of whole-grain breads. These dips and spreads are not only delicious, they are also highly nutritious. However, they are high in calories; so use them sparingly if you are trying to lose weight.

## ••••Bean Dip

*Makes 8 Servings (1/4 cup serving)*

| | |
|---|---|
| | 16-ounce can or 2 cups cooked cannellini or white kidney beans, drained and rinsed |
| 4 | large cloves garlic, boiled for 5 minutes, then peeled and sliced |
| 1 | tablespoon olive oil |
| 2 | teaspoons fresh lemon juice |
| 1/4 to 1/2 | teaspoon hot pepper sauce |
| 1 to 2 | teaspoons minced jalapeños (fresh or canned), or to taste |

Combine all the ingredients in a food processor, blending them until they are smooth.

*Exchanges per Serving:*
Vegetables: 1/8
Legumes: 1/2
Fats: 1/2

*Nutritional Information per Serving:*
Calories: 89
Carbohydrate: 64%
Protein: 22%
Fat: 14%
Fiber: 20 g
Calcium: 101 mg

*Comments:* Serve this dip with tortilla chips or firm vegetables such as celery, carrots, and bell peppers. It is a great dip for people suffering from elevated cholesterol levels.

◆◆◆◆

# •••• *Black Bean Spread*

*Makes 6 Servings (2 tablespoons per serving)*

| | |
|---|---|
| 2 | cups cooked black beans, drained |
| 1 | cup carrot, apple, lemon pulp |
| 1 | tablespoon creamy peanut butter |
| 1 | large clove garlic |
| 2 | scallions, chopped |
| 2 | tablespoons chopped cilantro |
| | Juice of 1 lime |
| | Pinch of Lite Salt or salt substitute |
| 1 | tablespoon green chili salsa |
| 1 | jalapeño, chopped (optional) |

In a blender or food processor, combine the beans, pulp, garlic, peanut butter, scallions, cilantro, half of the lime juice, and the Lite Salt or salt substitute. Blend until smooth. Transfer to a bowl, and add the rest of the lime and the green chili salsa. Garnish with cilantro and thin green and red pepper strips.

*Exchanges per Serving:*
Vegetables: 1/3          Legumes: 3/4
Fruits: 1/8              Fats: 1/2

*Nutritional Information per Serving:*
Calories: 105         Protein: 22%      Fiber: 39 g
Carbohydrate: 64%    Fat: 14%          Calcium: 54 mg

*Comments:* This is an excellent dip for Mexican foods, and it provides a convenient and tasty way to increase your consumption of legumes.

◆◆◆◆

# ••••*Eggplant Caviar*

*Makes 14 Servings (1/2 cup per serving)*

|       |                                            |
|-------|--------------------------------------------|
| 1     | teaspoon vegetable oil                     |
|       | Lite Salt or salt substitute               |
| 5     | medium eggplants                           |
| 1 1/4 | cups chopped fresh parsley                 |
| 5     | tablespoons white vinegar                  |
| 2 1/2 | tablespoons fresh lemon juice              |
| 2 1/2 | tablespoons crushed fresh mint leaves      |
| 2 1/2 | teaspoons Lite Salt or salt substitute     |
| 1 1/2 | teaspoons granulated garlic                |
| 1 1/4 | teaspoons freshly ground white pepper      |
| 3/4   | teaspoon ground cinnamon                   |

Preheat oven to 350°F. Oil a rimmed baking sheet, and sprinkle it with Lite Salt or salt substitute. Cut the eggplants in half lengthwise, and set them cut side down on the baking sheet. Bake until the eggplant is tender (about 45 minutes). Remove the eggplants from oven, and let them stand until cool enough to handle. Peel the eggplant, and finely chop the pulp. Transfer the pulp to a colander, and let it stand briefly to drain.

In a large bowl thoroughly combine the eggplant with the remaining ingredients. Cover and refrigerate for at least 24 hours. Adjust seasoning if necessary.

**Exchanges per Serving:**
Vegetables: 1
Fats: 1/14

**Nutritional Information per Serving:**

| Calories: 62       | Protein: 6% | Fiber: 0.9 g    |
|--------------------|-------------|-----------------|
| Carbohydrate: 65%  | Fat: 29%    | Calcium: 9 mg   |

*Comments:* This dip must be prepared at least 24 hours ahead, so that the flavors have time to mellow.

◆◆◆◆

# ◆◆◆◆ *Guacamole Dip*

*Makes 12 Servings (1 1/2 tablespoons per serving)*

| | |
|---|---|
| 1/2 | cup onion (preferably red onion), peeled and finely chopped |
| 3 | small firm tomatoes (plum tomatoes are best), finely diced |
| 2 | small jalapeños (2 tablespoons), seeded and minced, or to taste |
| 2 | tablespoons fresh lime juice |
| 1 | large clove garlic, peeled and minced |
| 2 | tablespoons finely chopped Italian parsley or 1 table-spoon cilantro |
| 1/2 | teaspoon Lite Salt or salt substitute |
| | Dash or more hot pepper sauce |
| 2 | large ripe avocados, peeled, pitted, and mashed |
| 2 | tablespoons pumpkin seeds (pepitas) |

Combine all of the ingredients in a medium-size bowl, placing the avocado pit in the center of the dip. Cover the bowl, and chill the guacamole until serving time.

*Exchanges per Serving:*
Vegetables: 1/4
Fruits: 1/12
Fats: 1

*Nutritional Information per Serving:*
Calories: 59
Carbohydrate: 16%
Protein: 7%
Fat: 77%
Fiber: 1 g
Calcium: 9 mg

**Comments:** Notice that this recipe contains no sour cream. As a result, the oils provided are predominantly health-promoting essential fatty acids.

◆◆◆◆

## ◆◆◆◆ *Hummus*

*Makes 16 Servings (2 tablespoons)*

|      |                                                                                         |
|------|-----------------------------------------------------------------------------------------|
|      | **15-ounce can or 1 2/3 cups cooked chick-peas, drained and with the liquid reserved** |
| 1/3  | **cup tahini (sesame paste)**                                                           |
| 1/3  | **cup lemon juice**                                                                     |
|      | **Water, if needed**                                                                    |
| 4    | **large cloves garlic, peeled and crushed**                                             |
| 1/2  | **teaspoon ground coriander**                                                           |
| 1/4  | **teaspoon cumin**                                                                      |
| 1/4  | **teaspoon paprika**                                                                    |
|      | **Dash cayenne**                                                                        |
| 1/4  | **cup minced scallions**                                                                |
| 2    | **tablespoons minced fresh parsley (for garnish)**                                      |

In a blender (in batches) or in a food processor, process the chick-peas, tahini, and lemon juice until the mixture reaches the consistency of a coarse paste; use as much of the chick-pea liquid and/or water as needed. Add the garlic, coriander, cumin, paprika, and cayenne, and process the ingredients again to combine them thoroughly. Transfer the hummus to a bowl, and stir in the scallions. Cover the hummus, and chill it until about 1 hour before serving time, adding the parsley garnish just before serving the dip.

*Exchanges per Serving:*
Vegetables: 1/16
Legumes: 1/4
Fats: 1/2

*Nutritional Information per Serving:*
Calories: 61
Carbohydrate: 54%
Protein: 15%
Fat: 41%
Fiber: 2 g
Calcium: 29 mg

**Comments:** Like the other bean dips, hummus is a great dip for people with heart disease. The combination of hummus and whole-wheat bread, has an excellent amino acid profile for complete proteins.

◆◆◆◆

# •••• Sun-dried Tomato Spread

*Makes 8 Servings (2 tablespoons per serving)*

| | |
|---|---|
| 1/4 | pound loose (dry) sun-dried tomatoes |
| | Warm water to cover |
| 2 | large cloves garlic, divided |
| 1 1/2 | tablespoons olive oil |
| 1/4 | teaspoon hot pepper flakes |
| 2 | bay leaves |
| 1/3 | cup packed grated Parmesan cheese |

Up to 2 weeks (and no less than 5 days) in advance, rinse the tomatoes to remove any debris, and place them in a bowl covered with warm water. Let them soak for 10 minutes; then drain them, and soak them again for another 10 minutes. Transfer the drained tomatoes to a vegetable steamer and steam them over boiling water for 7 minutes, or until they are plumped. Transfer the tomatoes to a clean, quart-size glass jar with a tight-fitting lid.

Peel and mince one clove of garlic, and add it—together with the oil, pepper flakes, and bay leaf—to the jar. Cover the jar tightly, and shake it to combine the ingredients thoroughly. Set the tomatoes aside for at least 5 days to marinate, shaking the jar once a day.

After 5 or more days, remove the bay leaf, and transfer the contents of the jar to a blender or food processor. Peel and mince the remaining clove of garlic, and add it and the Parmesan cheese to the tomato mixture. Blend the mixture until it is smooth.

*Exchanges per Serving:*
Vegetables: 1/8
Fats: 3/4
Meat: 1/2

*Nutritional Information per Serving:*
Calories: 100          Protein: 24%          Fiber: Trace
Carbohydrate: 6%       Fat: 70%              Calcium: 198 mg

*Comments:* This spread is great with bread and fresh pasta, and it offers a good way to get garlic into the diet.

◆◆◆◆

# ••••*Tofu Banana Nut Spread*

*Makes 4 Servings (2 tablespoons per serving)*

| | |
|---|---|
| 1/4 | cup nut butter (cashew-sunflower is good) |
| 8 | ounces silken tofu |
| 2 to 3 | tablespoons fresh lemon juice |
| 2 | tablespoons mellow red or white miso |
| 1 | large banana |
| 1 | tablespoon fruit sweetener |

Combine all the ingredients in a blender or food processor, and process until the spread is smooth and creamy. Refrigerate. This recipe makes about 1 1/2 cups. Great for kids.

*Exchanges per Serving:*
Fruits: 1/2            Legumes: 1/4          Fats: 3

*Nutritional Information per Serving:*
Calories: 312         Protein: 20%          Fiber: 8.1 g
Carbohydrate: 20%     Fat: 60%              Calcium: 220 mg

*Comments:* This spread is delicious with rice crackers, whole wheat bread, or pita bread.

◆◆◆◆

# ••••*Tofu-Sesame Dip*

*Makes 10 to 12 Servings (2 tablespoons per serving)*

|     |                                              |
|-----|----------------------------------------------|
| 3   | tablespoons cider vinegar                    |
| 3   | tablespoons water                            |
| 1   | tablespoon tamari or imported soy sauce      |
| 1   | tablespoon Chinese sesame oil                |
| 2   | small cloves garlic, peeled and crushed      |
| 1   | tablespoon lemon juice                       |
| 1   | cake (1/4 pound) tofu                        |
| 1/4 | cup tahini (sesame paste)                    |
| 1   | scallion, finely minced                      |
| 1/4 | cup packed minced fresh parsley              |
|     | Freshly ground pepper to taste               |
|     | Cayenne pepper to taste                      |

In a blender or food processor, purée the vinegar, water, tamari (or soy sauce), sesame oil, garlic, lemon juice, and tofu. Whisk the tahini in a bowl for a few minutes, and beat it into the purée. Stir into the mixture the scallion, parsley, pepper, and cayenne. Cover the dip, and chill it thoroughly before serving.

*Exchanges per Serving:*
Vegetables: 1/8                    Fats: 1 1/2

*Nutritional Information per Serving:*
Calories: 63                 Protein: 13%          Fiber: trace
Carbohydrate: 17%            Fat: 70%              Calcium: 50 mg

*Comments:* This dip is best served with fresh vegetables. It is a healthful alternative to many other vegetable dips.

••••

# 7

## ·····*Vegetables*

Vegetables provide the broadest range of nutritional and healing benefits of any food class. In Latin, the word *vegetable* means "to enliven or animate." Vegetables give us life. More and more evidence shows that a diet high in vegetables can prevent as well as treat many diseases. Obviously, vegetables should play a major role in your diet.

When cooking vegetables, be careful not to overcook them. Overcooking not only results in a loss of important nutrients; it also alters the flavor of the vegetable. Light steaming, baking, and quick stir-frying are the best ways to cook vegetables. Do not boil vegetables unless you are making soup, since many of the nutrients will be left in the water. If fresh vegetables are unavailable, choose frozen vegetables over their canned counterparts.

# ••••Cauliflower Creole

*Makes 4 Servings*

| | |
|---|---|
| 1/2 | cup water |
| 1 | head cauliflower |
| 1 | large onion, chopped |
| 1 | clove garlic, crushed |
| 1 | pound tomatoes, chopped |
| 1 | large green bell pepper, seeded and chopped |
| 1 | teaspoon Tabasco sauce |
| | Black pepper to taste |

Heat the water in a medium-size skillet. Add the onion and garlic, and cook for 2 to 3 minutes, until just tender. Stir in the tomatoes. Simmer gently, covered, for 10 minutes. Add the cauliflower and bell pepper, and simmer for approximately 20 minutes, until just tender. Season with Tabasco sauce and pepper. Pour a little sauce over the cauliflower, leaving some of the white flower showing. Pour the remaining sauce around the sides.

*Exchanges per Serving:*
Vegetables: 1 1/2

*Nutritional Information per Serving:*
Calories: 75
Protein: 17%
Carbohydrate: 75%
Fat: 8%
Fiber: 2 g
Calcium: 64 mg

*Comments:* If you haven't already found a way to enjoy cauliflower, give this recipe a try.

♦ ♦ ♦ ♦

# ••••*Country Brussels Sprouts*

*Makes 4 Servings*

| | |
|---|---|
| 1 1/2 | pounds brussels sprouts |
| 1 | cup water |
| 1 | large onion, sliced |
| 1 | green bell pepper, seeded and chopped |
| 1 | pound tomatoes, peeled and chopped |
| 1/2 | teaspoon dried basil |
| | Black pepper to taste |

Trim each brussels sprout, and cut a 1/8-inch-deep X in the base of each one. Steam the sprouts in a basket for 10 to 12 minutes, until just tender. Drain well. Meanwhile, in a large skillet, heat 1/2 cup of water over moderate heat. Cook the onion and green pepper until tender. Bring the remaining water to a boil, and pour it over the tomatoes. Let stand for 1 minute; then plunge the tomatoes into cold water. Add brussels sprouts, tomatoes, and basil to the skillet; and heat through. Season with pepper and serve immediately.

*Exchanges per Serving:*
Vegetables: 2

*Nutritional Information per Serving:*
Calories: 107
Protein: 18%
Carbohydrate: 73%
Fat: 9%
Fiber: 3 g
Calcium: 85 mg

*Comments:* This is another great recipe for making an often unpalatable vegetable extremely tasty.

••••

# ••••*Curried Potatoes*

*Makes 4 Servings*

| | |
|---|---|
| 1 | pound new potatoes, halved |
| 1 | small onion, sliced |
| 1/4 | teaspoon curry powder |
| 1 | tablespoon snipped fresh parsley |
| 1 | teaspoon fresh lemon juice |
| | Cayenne pepper to taste |

In a medium-size pot, boil the potatoes and onion, covered, for 15 minutes or until the potatoes are just tender; then drain. Meanwhile, in a small bowl, mix the curry powder, parsley, lemon juice, and pepper. Add the curry mixture to the potatoes and onion; toss gently to mix. Transfer to a serving dish.

*Exchanges per Serving:*
Vegetables: 1/8
Grains and starches: 1 1/2

*Nutritional Information per Serving:*
Calories: 105
Protein: 8%
Carbohydrate: 90%
Fat: 2%
Fiber: 1 g
Calcium: 16 mg

*Comments:* This simple, quick, and highly nutritious side dish is extremely versatile as an accompaniment to many other dishes.

••••

# ••••*Fennel and Mushrooms*

*Makes 6 Servings*

|       |                                                                                                          |
|-------|----------------------------------------------------------------------------------------------------------|
| 1     | tablespoon olive oil                                                                                     |
| 1     | clove garlic, peeled and sliced                                                                          |
| 1     | large tomato, peeled, seeded, and chopped                                                                |
| 2     | large bulbs fennel (1 or more pounds each), cored, trimmed of tops and stems, and thinly sliced lengthwise |
| 1     | pound mushrooms, sliced                                                                                  |
| 1/4   | cup hot vegetable stock                                                                                  |
| 1/2   | teaspoon dried basil or 1/4 teaspoon thyme                                                               |
| 1/2   | teaspoon or more Lite Salt or salt substitute, to taste (optional)                                      |
| 1/4 to 1/2 | teaspoon freshly ground black pepper, to taste                                                     |

In a large pan, heat the olive oil. Add the garlic, and cook it until it softens. Add the tomato and fennel, cover the pan, and simmer the ingredients for 5 minutes, stirring them often, or until the fennel is half-cooked. Add the mushrooms, broth, basil or thyme, Lite Salt or salt substitute (if desired), and pepper. Cover the pan, and simmer the mixture 5 to 10 minutes longer, or until the vegetables are tender but firm.

*Preparation tip:* This recipe can be prepared in advance through the step where the last ingredients are added. Do the final simmer just before serving the dish.

**Exchanges per Serving:**
Vegetables: 1                    Fats: 1/2

**Nutritional Information per Serving:**
Calories: 44             Protein: 20%        Fiber: 1.6 g
Carbohydrate: 53%        Fat: 27%            Calcium: 24 mg

*Comments:* Fennel is an absolutely delecious vegetable that most Americans have never tried.

◆◆◆◆

# ••••*Green Beans Amandine*

*Makes 6 Servings*

| | |
|---|---|
| 1 1/2 | pounds green beans, trimmed and slivered |
| 1/2 | cup vegetable stock or water |
| 1 | teaspoon olive oil (or butter) |
| 2 | cloves garlic, minced |
| 1/4 | cup slivered almonds |
| 1 | tablespoon chopped shallots or 1 small onion, chopped |

In a large skillet, combine the green beans and stock. Bring to a boil; then reduce heat and cook, covered, until tender (5 to 7 minutes). Drain the green beans and place them on a serving platter. Heat the olive oil (or butter) in a skillet, and add the garlic, almonds, and shallots. Sauté until the shallots are glazed and golden (do not brown). Add this to the green beans, and toss to coat well.

*Exchanges per Serving:*
Vegetables: 1                          Fats: 1

*Nutritional Information per Serving:*
Calories: 90                  Protein: 16%         Fiber: 2 g
Carbohydrate: 62%            Fat: 22%             Calcium: 69 mg

*Comments:* Green beans are fantastic diet foods—rich in nutrients, yet low in calories.

◆◆◆◆

# ••••Greens, Walnuts, and Raisins

*Makes 6 Servings*

| | |
|---|---|
| 2 | large bunches greens, washed, trimmed, and coarsely chopped |
| 1 | tablespoon olive oil |
| 1 | cup diced scallions |
| 1/3 | cup raisins |
| 1/2 | cup coarsely chopped walnuts |
| | Lite Salt or salt substitute, to taste |
| | Freshly ground pepper, to taste |
| | Lemon wedges |

Place the greens in a steamer over medium heat, and cook until just limp. Transfer to a bowl. Heat 1 tablespoon oil in a medium-size skillet over medium-high heat. Add the onion, raisins, and walnuts, and sauté until softened. Add these to the greens (additional oil if necessary) and toss to combine. Season with Lite Salt or salt substitute and pepper, to taste. Serve with lemon wedges.

*Exchanges per Serving:*
Vegetables: 1 1/2
Fruits: 1
Fats: 1/2

*Nutritional Information per Serving:*

| | | |
|---|---|---|
| Calories: 125 | Protein: 18% | Fiber: 2.3 g |
| Carbohydrate: 52% | Fat: 30% | Calcium: 30 mg |

*Comments:* This is a great way to eat greens such as spinach, kale, and mustard greens.

♦ ♦ ♦ ♦

# ····*Herbed Green Bean–Zucchini Combo*

*Makes 6 Servings*

| | |
|---|---|
| 1/2 | pound green beans, sliced diagonally into 1-inch pieces |
| 2 | small zucchini, sliced |
| 1/4 | cup chopped green bell pepper |
| 2 | tablespoons chopped onion |
| 1/2 | cup water |
| 1 | medium tomato, chopped |
| 1/4 | teaspoon dried thyme, crushed |
| 1/4 | teaspoon dried rosemary, crushed |
| | Black pepper to taste |

Steam the green beans in a basket for 10 minutes, or until tender-crisp. Add the zucchini; cover and steam for 12 to 15 minutes more, or until the vegetables are tender. Meanwhile, in a small pot, cook the green pepper and onion in the water until tender. Stir in the tomato, thyme, rosemary, and pepper; and heat through. Pour this mixture over the green beans and zucchini in a serving bowl, and toss gently.

**Exchanges per Serving:**
Vegetables: 1/2

**Nutritional Information per Serving:**

| | | |
|---|---|---|
| Calories: 27 | Protein: 19% | Fiber: 1 g |
| Carbohydrate: 74% | Fat: 7% | Calcium: 29 mg |

**Comments:** Notice the calories per serving.

◆ ◆ ◆ ◆

# ••••*Leek and Tomato Casserole*

*Makes 4 Servings*

| | |
|---|---|
| 2 | large leeks, tops and tails trimmed |
| 2 | large onions, cut into eighths |
| | 14-ounce can low-sodium tomatoes |
| 1 | tablespoon chopped fresh parsley |
| 1 | bay leaf |
| 2 | cloves garlic, crushed |
| 2/3 | cup homemade vegetable stock |
| 1 | tablespoon fresh lemon juice |
| | Dried thyme to taste |
| | Black pepper to taste |

Slit each leek down almost to the base, and fan it under cold running water to rinse off any remaining dirt. Cut into 1-inch pieces. Preheat oven to 350°F. In a large bowl, mix all the ingredients well. Turn the mixture into a large baking dish or casserole dish. Bake, covered, 1 1/2 to 2 hours, until tender. Serve hot.

*Exchanges per Serving:*
Vegetables: 2

*Nutritional Information per Serving:*
Calories: 90
Protein: 12%
Carbohydrate: 82%
Fat: 6%
Fiber: 2 g
Calcium: 90 mg

*Comments:* If you like leeks, you'll love this recipe. It's great for lowering blood pressure and cholesterol levels.

••••

# ••••*Lemon Carrots*

*Makes 4 Servings*

| | |
|---|---|
| 6 | medium carrots, quartered |
| 1 | tablespoon fresh lemon juice |
| 1/8 | teaspoon ground nutmeg |
| 1 | tablespoon snipped fresh parsley |

Steam the carrots in a basket for 12 to 15 minutes, until tender-crisp; then set aside. Mix the lemon juice and nutmeg; add this to carrots, and toss gently. Turn the mixture into individual serving bowls, and sprinkle with parsley.

*Exchanges per Serving:*
Vegetables: 1

*Nutritional Information per Serving:*
Calories: 50
Protein: 9%
Carbohydrate: 87%
Fat: 4%
Fiber: 1 g
Calcium: 26 mg

*Comments:* Quick, easy, and extremely versatile. The nutmeg and lemon give this dish a unique flavor.

◆ ◆ ◆ ◆

# ···· *Marinated Artichokes*

*Makes 2 Servings*

*Vegetable*

| | |
|---|---|
| 2 | artichokes, cooked |

*Marinade*

| | |
|---|---|
| 1/2 | cup orange juice |
| 1/8 | cup olive oil |
| 2 | tablespoons tarragon vinegar |
| 2 | tablespoons chopped shallot or scallion |
| 1 | tablespoon minced fresh parsley |
| 1 1/2 | teaspoons grated orange peel |
| 1/2 | teaspoon Lite Salt or salt substitute |
| | Pinch each of tarragon, basil, and chervil |
| 1/4 | teaspoon dry mustard |
| 1/4 | teaspoon Worcestershire sauce |

Cut the artichokes in half, from tip to stem. Remove the choke and the small inner leaves. Combine all ingredients for the marinade in a medium-size bowl, and blend well. Add the artichokes, turning them several times to coat. Cover and refrigerate overnight. Serve the artichokes with some of the marinade spooned over the top.

**Exchanges per Serving:**

| Vegetables: 1 | Fruits: 1/2 | Fats: 4 |
|---|---|---|

**Nutritional Information per Serving:**

| Calories: 199 | Protein: 11% | Fiber: 1.7 g |
|---|---|---|
| Carbohydrate: 60% | Fat: 29% | Calcium: 87 mg |

**Comments:** This is a great dish to serve when entertaining.

◆◆◆◆

# •••• *Mashed Potatoes and Onion Gravy*

*Makes 6 Servings*

*Vegetable*

| | |
|---|---|
| 4 | medium potatoes, boiled and mashed |

*Gravy*

| | |
|---|---|
| 1 | cup sliced onion, separated into rings |
| 1 | cup water |
| 1 3/4 | teaspoons cornstarch |
| 1/8 | teaspoon Lite Salt or salt substitute |
| 1/8 | teaspoon pepper |
| | Vegetable cooking spray |

To prepare the gravy, first coat a medium-size skillet with cooking spray, and place the skillet over medium heat until hot. Add the onion slices, and sauté until soft and lightly browned. Combine the water, cornstarch, Lite Salt or salt substitute, and pepper; stir well, and add to the onion in the skillet. Bring to a boil, and cook for 1 minute, stirring constantly. Pour liberally over the mashed potatoes.

*Exchanges per Serving:*
Vegetables: 1/6                          Grains and starches: 1

*Nutritional Information per Serving:*
Calories: 78                   Protein: 8%          Fiber: 1.6 g
Carbohydrate: 90%        Fat: 2%               Calcium: 38 mg

*Comments:* This is a very healthful way to eat potatoes and gravy.

•••

# •••• Medley of Artichoke and Asparagus

*Makes 6 Servings*

| | |
|---|---|
| 1/2 | pound fresh asparagus spears |
| 1 | can artichoke hearts (water pack) |
| 1/2 | cup sliced fresh mushrooms |
| 1/4 | cup sliced scallion |
| 1 | tablespoon blackberry or raspberry vinegar |
| 1 | teaspoon toasted sesame seeds |
| 6 | leaves Romaine lettuce |
| | Tabasco to taste |

Steam the asparagus in a basket until tender-crisp. In a 10 × 6 × 2-inch dish, arrange the asparagus spears. Drain the artichoke hearts. Slice any large artichoke hearts in half, and combine the hearts with the mushrooms and onion. Add this mixture to dish. In a small bowl, combine the vinegar, sesame seeds, and Tabasco. Pour this over the mixture, and toss. Allow the vegetables to marinate for 15 minutes. Then arrange the vegetables on individual lettuce-lined plates.

*Exchanges per Serving:*
Vegetables: 1
Fats: 1/6

*Nutritional Information per Serving:*

| | |
|---|---|
| Calories: 44 | Fat: 12% |
| Carbohydrate: 63% | Fiber: 1 g |
| Protein: 25% | Calcium: 48 mg |

**Comments:** This dish is also delicious when chilled.

••••

# ••••*Southern Succotash*

*Makes 4 Servings*

| | |
|---|---|
| 1 | medium onion, very finely chopped |
| 1/3 | cup water |
| 1 | cup corn kernels (approximately 3 ears), fresh or frozen |
| 1 | pound zucchini, unpeeled, quartered lengthwise, and cut crosswise into 1/2-inch slices |
| 1 | pint cherry tomatoes, halved, or 28-ounce can plum tomatoes, drained and quartered |
| 1 | teaspoon dried oregano |
| | Black pepper to taste |

In a large skillet, sauté the onion in the water until tender. Add the corn, zucchini, tomatoes, oregano, and pepper, tossing the ingredients to combine them. Cook, covered, over moderately low heat for 15 minutes, stirring gently a few times. Transfer to a serving dish.

*Exchanges per Serving:*
Vegetables: 2

*Nutritional Information per Serving:*

| | |
|---|---|
| Calories: 100 | Fat: 4% |
| Protein: 16% | Fiber: 1 g |
| Carbohydrate: 80% | Calcium: 21 mg |

*Comments:* This variation of the Southern classic is extremely easy to prepare and quick to cook.

♦♦♦♦

# •••• Spiced Yams

*Makes 8 to 10 Servings*

|     |                                            |
| --- | ------------------------------------------ |
| 4   | pounds yams                                |
| 1/4 | cup unsalted butter, room temperature      |
| 1/2 | teaspoon allspice                          |
| 1/2 | teaspoon cinnamon                          |
| 1/4 | teaspoon nutmeg                            |
| 1/4 | teaspoon ground ginger                     |
|     | Pinch of ground cloves                     |
|     | Lite Salt or salt substitute               |
|     | Freshly ground pepper                      |
| 1   | tablespoon minced fresh parsley (garnish)  |

Preheat oven to 400°F. Generously grease a baking dish. Make a 2-inch slit in the center of each yam, and bake them until soft (about 1 1/4 hours). Remove them from oven, reduce oven temperature to 350°F, and let the yams stand until cool enough to handle (about 20 minutes). Halve them lengthwise, and scoop the pulp into a large mixing bowl. Discard the skins. Add all of the remaining ingredients, except the parsley, and beat well. Taste and adjust the seasoning. Turn the yams into a soufflé dish, and dot them with additional butter. Bake uncovered until the top is lightly browned (about 1 hour). Sprinkle with minced parsley before serving.

*Exchanges per Serving:*
Grains and starches: 2
Fats: 1

*Nutritional Information per Serving:*

| | |
|---|---|
| Calories: 185 | Fat: 30% |
| Carbohydrate: 61% | Fiber: 0.19 g |
| Protein: 19% | Calcium: 21.7 mg |

*Comments:* Yams should be consumed on a regular basis, because of their excellent nutritional profile. They are especially rich in carotenes. Unfortunately, most Americans only consume yams at Thanksgiving.

◆◆◆◆

# ◆◆◆◆ *Spicy Hot Leeks*

*Makes 4 Servings*

| | |
|---|---|
| 2 | pounds leeks (approximately 6 to 8), trimmed of green tops |
| 1/2 | cup water |
| 1/4 | teaspoon cayenne pepper |
| 2 | medium tomatoes, peeled, seeded, and chopped |
| 2 | cloves garlic, minced |
| 1/4 | teaspoon ground allspice |
| 1 | tablespoon chopped fresh basil |
| | Juice of 1/2 lemon |
| 2 | tablespoons chopped fresh parsley |

In a large skillet, heat the water over medium heat. Add the leeks in one layer. As the water starts to bubble, turn the leeks over, and sprinkle them with pepper. Cook for 1 minute. Reduce heat to medium-low. Cook, covered, until the leeks are tender (12 to 15 minutes). Transfer them to a serving dish; keep it warm. Add the tomatoes to the skillet, and cook over high heat for 1 minute. Add the garlic, allspice, and basil. Cook for 1 minute more. Add the lemon juice and 1 tablespoon of the parsley. Stir to mix, and spoon over leeks. Sprinkle with the remaining parsley. This dish is good hot or cold.

**Exchanges per Serving:**
Vegetables: 3

*Nutritional Information per Serving:*
Calories: 146           Protein: 7%           Fiber: 3 g
Carbohydrate: 63%       Fat: 30%              Calcium: 111 mg

*Comments:* A spicy way to include leeks, garlic, cayenne
pepper, and their health-promoting properties in your diet.

◆ ◆ ◆ ◆

# ◆◆◆◆ *Steamed Kale*

*Makes 4 Servings*

    1    pound kale
    1    teaspoon virgin olive oil
    2    large cloves garlic, minced
    1/4  cup water

To prepare kale, cut off and discard the tough stems, slice the
leaves once down the middle, and then cut them crosswise
into 1-inch-wide strips. In a large pot, heat the oil. Add the
garlic and cook, stirring frequently, for 15 seconds (do not
brown). Add the water and bring the mixture to a boil. Add
the kale to the mixture, and steam, covered, for 5 minutes or
until the kale is just tender but still bright green. Toss to mix
well. Transfer to a serving dish.

*Exchanges per Serving:*
Vegetables: 1                    Fats: 1/4

*Nutritional Information per Serving:*
Calories: 58            Protein: 25%          Fiber: 1 g
Carbohydrate: 55%       Fat: 20%              Calcium: 85 mg

*Comments:* Kale is extremely rich in calcium, other minerals,
and vitamin K. It is a great food for healthy bones.

◆ ◆ ◆ ◆

# ••••Stir-fried Vegetables

*Makes 8 Servings*

| | |
|---|---|
| 2 | tablespoons minced ginger root |
| 1/4 | head cauliflower, separated into florets |
| 1/4 | pound broccoli, separated into florets |
| 1/2 | cup julienne-cut celery |
| 1/4 | pound pea pods |
| 1/4 | head Napa cabbage, shredded |
| 10 | mushrooms, diced |
| 1/4 | pound bamboo shoots, diced |
| 1 | tablespoon low-sodium soy sauce |
| 1/2 | cup thinly sliced water chestnuts |
| 1 | medium onion, thinly sliced |
| 1/4 | pound bean sprouts |

In a heated wok or skillet, add ginger root, cauliflower, broccoli, celery, and pea pods. Stir-fry for 2 minutes over high heat. Add cabbage, mushrooms, and bamboo shoots. Stir-fry for 1 minute more. Stir in soy sauce, and simmer over low heat for 1 minute. Add water chestnuts, onion, and bean sprouts, and stir-fry for 1 minute over high heat until tender-crisp.

**Exchanges per Serving:**
Vegetables: 1                    Fats: 1/8

**Nutritional Information per Serving:**
Calories: 45            Protein: 25%          Fiber: 1 g
Carbohydrate: 69%       Fat: 6%               Calcium: 37 mg

*Comments:* Stir-frying vegetables is perhaps the quickest way to cook them (microwaving excluded). Don't overcook the vegetables, as this would cause the loss of much nutritional value.

◆◆◆◆

# •••• *Stuffed Mushrooms with Feta and Dill*

*Makes 4 Servings*

| | |
|---|---|
| 1/4 | cup walnuts, chopped |
| 1/3 | cup bread crumbs (whole wheat) |
| 1 | tablespoon dill |
| 1/3 | cup finely crumbled feta cheese |
| 2 | tablespoons soy milk |
| | Ground pepper |
| 16 | large mushrooms |
| 1 | teaspoon olive oil |

Preheat oven to 375°F. Mix the walnuts, bread crumbs, dill, feta, soy milk, and pepper together in a medium-size bowl. Clean the mushrooms and remove the stems. Stuff each mushroom cap with the bread crumb mixture. Place the mushrooms in a baking dish, and brush them lightly with olive oil. Bake for 20 minutes or until brown.

*Exchanges per Serving:*
Vegetables: 1/2          Fats: 1
Grains and starches: 1/2      Milk: 1/4

*Nutritional Information per Serving:*
Calories: 130           Fat: 30%
Carbohydrate: 35%        Fiber: 0.5 g
Protein: 35%           Calcium: 161 mg

*Comments:* This is a great appetizer to serve when entertaining.

◆ ◆ ◆ ◆

# ••••*Stuffed Onions*

*Makes 6 Servings*

| | |
|---|---|
| 3 | Walla Walla sweet onions (each 3 1/2 to 4 inches in diameter), peeled |
| 3 | medium carrots, thinly sliced |
| | Pinch of Lite Salt or salt substitute |
| 1 | pound fresh spinach, well washed and trimmed |
| 1/2 | teaspoon herb or vegetable salt |
| 1 | tablespoon olive oil (preferably cold-pressed) |
| 1 | teaspoon minced fresh garlic |
| 1/2 | cup golden or dark raisins, plumped in white wine or water and drained |
| 1/4 | cup walnuts |
| 3/4 | cup sour cream (optional) |
| 3 | tablespoons freshly grated Parmesan cheese |
| 1 1/2 | tablespoons dry whole wheat breadcrumbs |

Combine onions and herb or vegetable salt in a large saucepan with enough water to cover. Bring to boil over medium-low heat, and let boil until the onions are just softened (about 2 minutes). Drain well; pat dry with paper towels. Cut in half crosswise. Using the tip of a small corer, carefully remove the centers, leaving the three outermost layers for a shell. Arrange the shells upright in baking dish. Finely chop the onion centers, and set these aside for later use.

Place the carrots and a pinch of Lite Salt or salt substitute in a small saucepan, and add just enough water to cover them. Bring to a boil over medium-low heat; drain quickly and set aside. Place the spinach in a large saucepan, and sprinkle with a pinch of Lite Salt or salt substitute. Sprinkle lightly with water. Cover and cook over high heat, turning the spinach frequently, until wilted (about 5 minutes). Transfer to colander and drain well, pressing with back of spoon or squeezing dry to remove as much excess moisture as possible. Cut the spinach into coarse shreds.

Heat oil in a large skillet over medium heat. Add the chopped onion and garlic, and sauté until the onion is soft but not brown. Add the carrots, raisins, and walnuts, and continue cooking until the carrots are almost tender. Increase heat to high, add the spinach, and cook for 2 minutes, stirring constantly. Remove from heat and let cool slightly. Stir in the sour cream. Taste and adjust seasoning.

Preheat broiler. Divide the mixture among the onions. Combine the cheese and breadcrumbs, and sprinkle over the tops. Broil until the tops are lightly golden (about 3 minutes), watching carefully to prevent burning. Serve immediately. The onions can be filled several hours ahead and refrigerated. Warm in 325°F oven, and then broil until the tops are lightly browned.

*Exchanges per Serving:*
Vegetables: 2
Fruits: 1/2
Grains and starches: 1/3
Fats: 2

*Nutritional Information per Serving:*
Calories: 217
Carbohydrate: 54%
Protein: 20%
Fat: 26%
Fiber: 4.1 g
Calcium: 173 mg

*Comments:* The key to this recipe is the Walla Walla onion. Although other large yellow onions can be used, the Walla Walla onion is particularly sweet.

◆◆◆◆

# •••• *Vegetable Curry*

*Makes 4 Servings*

| | |
|---|---|
| 1 | small onion, chopped |
| 1 | clove garlic, crushed |
| 1 | tart apple, peeled and diced |
| 2 | teaspoon curry powder |
| 2 | teaspoons oil |
| 2 | medium carrots, peeled and diced |
| 1 1/3 | cup diced yellow squash or zucchini |
| 2/3 | cup uncooked brown rice |
| 1/2 | cup raisins |
| 2 | vegetarian bouillon cubes |
| 2 | cups water |
| 1 | tablespoon lemon juice |
| 1/2 | cup frozen peas, thawed |
| 1/2 | cup coarsely chopped roasted nuts |

In a large heavy saucepan, sauté the onion, garlic, apple, and curry in oil for 5 minutes. Add the carrot, squash, and rice. Cook about 5 minutes longer. Add the raisins, bouillon, water and lemon juice. Bring to a boil. Cover and simmer for about 45 minutes, or until the rice is tender and the liquid is absorbed. Stir in the peas. Heat through. Sprinkle with nuts.

*Exchanges per Serving:*
Vegetables: 1                    Grains and starches: 1/2
Fruits: 3/4                      Fats: 2

*Nutritional Information per Serving:*
Calories: 204          Protein: 7%          Fiber: 9 g
Carbohydrate: 70%      Fat: 23%             Calcium: 71 mg

*Comments:* Curries provide a wide range of spices that add flavor and valuable medicinal properties.

•••

# ••••  *Vegetables Italiano*

*Makes 4 Servings*

| | |
|---|---|
| 1/4 | cup chopped onion |
| 1 | clove garlic, minced |
| 1/4 | cup water |
| 1 | medium zucchini, sliced |
| 1 | cup frozen whole kernel corn, thawed |
| 1 | small green bell pepper, cut into strips |
| 1/2 | teaspoon dried basil |
| 1/2 | teaspoon dried oregano |
| 1/4 | teaspoon black pepper |
| 1 | small tomato, cut into wedges |

In a medium-size skillet, cook the onion and garlic in the water until the onion is tender. Stir in the zucchini, corn, green pepper, basil, oregano, and pepper. Cook over medium heat, stirring frequently, for 5 minutes or until the zucchini is tender-crisp. Stir in the tomato. Cook, covered, for 1 minute more or until the tomato is heated through. Serve immediately.

*Exchanges per Serving:*
Vegetables: 1

*Nutritional Information per Serving:*
Calories: 48                     Fat: 5%
Carbohydrate: 80%          Fiber: 1 g
Protein: 15%                    Calcium: 20 mg

*Comments:* This is a great vegetable side dish with pasta or pizza.

••••

# 8

# ••••*Grains and Legumes*

Whole grains and legumes are low in calories, high in fiber, and high in complex carbohydrates. Since cooking grains and legumes in water tremendously increases their water content, this along with the foods' high fiber content provides incredible bulking action. In other words, whole grains and legumes promote healthy bowel function and are quite filling. The latter effect is of great importance in reducing calorie intake. Whole grains and legumes also promote healthy liver and gallblader function, help lower cholesterol levels, and lessen the risk for certain types of cancer. The whole-grain and legume recipes in this chapter include some that can be used as breakfast cereals, as side dishes, or as entrées.

## Guidelines for Cooking
## Grains and Legumes

Whole grains are very easy to prepare: simply rinse the grain to remove any debris; bring the water to a boil in an appropriate-size saucepan; stir in the grain; reduce the heat; simmer, covered, for the suggested cooking time; and test for doneness.

To prepare dried legumes, first rinse them, to remove any debris, and then soak them overnight in an appropriate amount of water (see Table 8.1). This is best done in the refrigerator, to prevent fermentation. Soaking usually cuts the required cooking time dramatically. To check to see whether the legume is done, simply let a few cool and taste them. They should be firm, but not crunchy. In addition, look to see whether some of the beans have split skins; too many split skins may indicate that the legume has been overcooked. If soaking overnight is not possible, here is an alternative method: place the dried legumes in an appropriate amount of water in a pot; for each cup of dried legumes, add 1/4 teaspoon of baking soda; bring to a boil for at least 2 minutes; then set aside to soak for at least 1 hour. The baking soda softens the

**Table 8.1** Yields of Cooked Grains and Legumes

| Grain or Legume (1 cup dry) | Water | Cooking | Yield |
|---|---|---|---|
| Baby limas | 2 cups | 1 1/2 hours | 1 3/4 cups |
| Barley | 3 cups | 1 1/4 hours | 3 1/2 cups |
| Black beans | 4 cups | 1 1/2 hours | 2 cups |
| Black-eyed peas | 3 cups | 1 hour | 2 cups |
| Brown rice | 2 cups | 45 minutes | 3 cups |
| Buckwheat (kasha) | 2 cups | 15 minutes | 2 1/2 cups |
| Bulgur wheat | 2 cups | 15 to 20 minutes | 2 1/2 cups |
| Cornmeal (polenta) | 4 cups | 25 minutes | 3 cups |
| Cracked wheat | 2 cups | 25 minutes | 2 1/3 cups |
| Garbanzos (chick-peas) | 2 cups | 3 hours | 2 cups |
| Great northern beans | 3 1/2 cups | 2 hours | 2 cups |
| Kidney beans | 3 cups | 1 1/2 hours | 2 cups |
| Lentils and split peas | 3 cups | 1 hour | 2 1/4 cups |
| Limas | 2 cups | 1 1/2 hour | 1 1/4 cups |
| Millet | 3 cups | 45 minutes | 3 1/2 cups |
| Pinto beans | 3 cups | 2 1/2 hours | 2 cups |
| Quinoa | 2 1/4 cups | 20 minutes | 2 cups |
| Red beans | 3 cups | 3 hours | 2 cups |
| Small white beans (navy) | 2 cups | 1 1/2 hours | 2 cups |
| Soybeans | 3 cups | 3 hours | 2 cups |
| Soy grits | 4 cups | 15 minutes | 2 cups |
| Whole wheat berries | 3 cups | 2 hours | 2 2/3 cups |
| Wild rice | 3 cups | 1 hour | 4 cups |

legumes and helps break down the troublesome oligosaccharides that cause flatulence. The baking soda also reduces the amount of cooking time required. After soaking, the beans should be simmered with a minimum of stirring, to keep them firm and unbroken. For convenience, a pressure cooker or crock pot may be used.

# ••••  *Black Bean Dal*

*Makes 6 servings*

| | |
|---|---|
| 1 1/2 | cups black beans |
| 6 | cups water |
| 1/4 | cup olive oil or canola oil |
| 1 | small garlic clove, chopped |
| 2 | teaspoons cumin seed |
| 1 | teaspoon ground coriander |
| 1 | teaspoon turmeric |
| 1 | teaspoon paprika |
| 1/2 | teaspoon ground ginger |
| | Lite Salt or salt substitute |
| | Ground red pepper |

Rinse the beans in a colander under cold running water. Drain well. Transfer to a 6- to 8-quart pot. Add the water and bring to a boil over high heat, skimming and discarding the forma as it accumulates on the surface. Add the oil, garlic, spices, salt, and red pepper. Reduce heat to low, cover the pot, and simmer until the beans are tender (about 1 hour). The mixture should have the consistency of thick soup. The recipe can be prepared ahead and refrigerated for 5 to 6 days. Reheat before serving. Serve hot with rice or bread.

*Exchanges per Serving:*
Legumes: 2
Fats: 1 1/2

*Nutritional Information per Serving:*
Calories: 200
Carbohydrate: 57%
Protein: 14%
Fat: 29%
Fiber: 6 g
Calcium: 59 mg

*Comments:* Another valuable recipe that lowers cholesterol levels and improves blood-sugar control.

◆◆◆◆

# ◆◆◆◆ *Black-eyed Peas and Brown Rice*

*Makes 6 Servings*

| | |
|---|---|
| 1 | cup dried black-eyed peas, picked over, rinsed, soaked 10 hours or longer in water to cover (by at least 4 inches), and drained |
| 5 | cups water, divided |
| 1 | cup basmati rice or long-grain brown rice |
| 1 | tablespoon canola oil or olive oil |
| 1 1/2 | cups finely chopped onions |
| 2 | large cloves garlic, peeled and minced |
| 1 | tablespoon grated or minced ginger |
| 1 | tablespoon diced green chili or jalapeño, fresh or canned, seeded |
| 1 | teaspoon molasses |

The peas and rice must be cooked simulataneously. In a medium-size saucepan, cook the presoaked peas in 3 cups of the water for 40 minutes. Add 1/2 teaspoon of the salt (if desired), and cook the peas for another 20 minutes or until they are tender. Drain the peas, saving 1/4 cup of the cooking liquid. Set the peas and the reserved cooking liquid aside.

In another medium-size saucepan, combine the rice and the remaining 2 cups of water. Bring the rice to a boil, reduce the heat to low, cover the saucepan, and simmer the rice for 35 to 40 minutes. When the water is fully absorbed and the rice is tender, turn off the heat and let the pan sit, covered, on the stove.

After the peas and rice have cooked for 15 minutes, in a large, heavy skillet (preferably one with a nonstick surface), heat the oil; add the onions, garlic, ginger, and chili or jalapeño; and sauté the vegetables over medium-high heat for 5 minutes. Reduce the heat to medium-low. Add the peas, the remaining 1/4 teaspoon of salt (if desired), the molasses, and, if needed, more liquid. Cook the mixture, stirring it occasionally, for 20 minutes. Serve the peas with the cooked rice.

*Exchanges per Serving:*
Vegetables: 1/6
Fruits: 1/6
Grains and starches: 1/3
Legumes: 1/3

*Nutritional Information per Serving:*

| | |
|---|---|
| Calories: 58 | Fat: 29% |
| Carbohydrate: 61% | Fiber: 2.5 g |
| Protein: 10% | Calcium: 16.3 mg |

*Comments:* For a less spicy version, prepare the recipe without the ginger and jalapeño.

◆◆◆◆

# ••••*Breton Beans*

*Makes 6 Servings*

*Beans*

| | |
|---|---|
| 2 | cups dried white navy beans, picked over, rinsed, soaked 10 hours in water to cover (by at least 4 inches), and drained |
| 8 | cups water |
| | Salt to taste (optional) |
| | Freshly ground black pepper to taste |
| 1 | carrot |
| 1 | onion, peeled and studded with 2 whole cloves |
| 1 | bay leaf |
| 1 | clove garlic, peeled |
| 2 | sprigs parsley |
| 1/4 | cup chopped fresh parsley for garnish |

*Tomato Sauce*

| | |
|---|---|
| 1 | tablespoon olive oil |
| 1 | cup finely chopped onion (1 large) |
| 1 | tablespoon minced garlic (3 large cloves) |
| 2 | cups crushed fresh or canned tomatoes |
| 2 | sprigs fresh thyme, chopped, or 1/2 teaspoon dried thyme |
| | Salt to taste (optional) |
| | Freshly ground black pepper to taste |

Place the presoaked beans in a large saucepan, and add the water, salt (if desired), pepper, carrot, clove-studded onion, bay leaf, garlic, and parsley sprigs. Bring the mixture to a boil, reduce the heat, and simmer the beans for 1 hour or until they are tender but not mushy. Do not overcook them.

While the beans are cooking, prepare the sauce. Heat the olive oil in a large skillet, add the onion and garlic, and sauté the vegetables until the onion is translucent. Add the tomatoes, thyme, salt (if desired), and pepper. Bring the sauce to a simmer, and cook it for 15 minutes.

When the beans are done, drain them, reserving 1 cup of the cooking liquid and discarding the carrot, onion, bay leaf, garlic, and parsley sprigs. Add the beans and the reserved cooking liquid to the tomato sauce. Adjust the seasonings. Bring the mixture to a boil, reduce the heat, and simmer the beans for 15 minutes. Serve the beans sprinkled with chopped parsley.

*Exchanges per Serving:*
Vegetables: 1/3
Legumes: 3/4
Fats: 3/4

*Nutritional Information per Serving:*
Calories: 88
Carbohydrate: 61%
Protein: 20%
Fat: 19%
Fiber: 2.5 g
Calcium: 43 mg

*Comments:* If you plan to use this dish as a main course, serve it with mashed potatoes or brown rice to form a complete protein.

◆◆◆

# ••••*Calico Rice*

*Makes 4 Servings*

1 1/2   cups basmati or brown rice
   2   cups vegetable and citrus pulp (optional)
   2   tablespoons blended spices: Lite Salt or salt substi-
      tute, pepper, thyme, basil, marjoram, sage, and
      savory
   2   cups water
   1   small onion, chopped
   1   green pepper, chopped
   1   medium tomato, chopped
   2   teaspoons olive oil

In a medium-size saucepan, combine the uncooked rice, pulp, and seasonings. Add water, bring to a boil, stir, and cover. Cook over medium heat for 25 to 30 minutes, or until the rice is tender. In a medium-size skillet, add the olive oil and sauté the onion and pepper for 2 minutes. Add the tomato and sauté for 2 to 3 minutes more. Set aside. When the rice is tender, add the sautéed vegetables; stir; and cook for 10 minutes more. Serve immediately

*Exchanges per Serving:*
Vegetables: 1/2                    Grains and starches: 3/4
Fruits: 1/4                        Fats: 1/2

*Nutritional Information per Serving:*
Calories: 91            Protein: 7%        Fiber: 1.6
Carbohydrate: 68%       Fat: 25%           Calcium: 12.5 mg

*Comments:* This recipe is a good example of how the pulp from a juice extractor can be recycled into foods. Virtually any vegetable pulp left over from juicing can be used; orange pulp works best for fruit pulp. A 1:1 vegetable-to-fruit ratio for the pulps is recommended.

••••

# •••• *Country-style Rice*

*Makes 4 Servings*

|  |  |
|--|--|
| 1 | teaspoon olive oil |
| 1 | onion, finely chopped |
| 1 | large carrot, finely chopped |
| 1 | celery stalk, finely chopped |
| 2 | medium zucchini, diced |
| 1/2 | cup shelled fresh peas |
| 1 1/2 | cups short-grain brown rice |
| 5 | cups hot vegetable stock (approximately) |
| 2 | tablespoons fresh parsley, chopped |
| 1/2 | cup freshly grated Parmesan cheese (optional) |

Heat the oil in a heavy-based saucepan, add all the vegetables, and stir them constantly until they begin to soften. Add the rice and stir it so that the grains are well coated with the oil. Stir in about two-thirds of the hot stock, cover the pan, and cook over very low heat, adding more hot stock from time to time until the rice is tender but still firm and creamy rather than mushy. After about 40 minutes, when the rice is cooked, remove the pan from the heat. Stir in the parsley and the Parmesan cheese. Adjust the seasoning. Turn onto a warmed serving dish and serve immediately.

*Exchanges per Serving:*

| | |
|--|--|
| Vegetables: 2 | Fats: 1/2 |
| Grains and starches: 3/4 | Milk: 1/2 |

*Nutritional Information per Serving:*

| | | |
|--|--|--|
| Calories: 203 | Protein: 19% | Fiber: 5.3 g |
| Carbohydrate: 55% | Fat: 26% | Calcium: 251 mg |

**Comments:** This is a nice recipe for people who prefer "American-style" food.

••••

# •••• *Curried Garbanzos with Peppers*

*Makes 4 Servings*

| | |
|---|---|
| 1 | teaspoon olive oil |
| 1 | clove garlic |
| 1/4 | cup chopped onion |
| 1 | medium green pepper, sliced thin |
| | Dash of freshly ground pepper |
| 1/2 | teaspoon basil (dried) |
| 1/2 | tablespoon chili powder |
| 1/8 | teaspoon cumin |
| 1/8 | teaspoon coriander |
| | Dash of dry mustard |
| 1 | cup vegetable juice (carrot, tomato, celery, spinach, parsley) |
| 1 | cup cooked garbanzos |

Heat the oil in a medium skillet. Mince the garlic and sauté it with the onion and green pepper until they are soft. Season with ground pepper and the remaining spices. Add the vegetable juice, and cook for about 5 minutes. Add the cooked garbanzos (follow the guide in Table 8.1), and heat through. For a thicker mixture, mash a few garbanzos with the back of a fork and blend in.

*Exchanges per Serving:*
Vegetables: 1/2      Legumes: 1              Fats: 1/4

*Nutritional Information per Serving:*
Calories: 99         Carbohydrate: 58%      Fiber: 3 g
Protein: 12%         Fat: 30%               Calcium: 26 mg

*Comments:* A low-sodium canned vegetable juice cocktail can be used in place of fresh juice, if desired.

♦ ♦ ♦ ♦

# •••• *Granola-like Breakfast*

*Makes 4 Servings*

|   |   |
|---|---|
| 4 | cups rolled oats |
| 4 | tablespoons sesame seeds (ground) |
| 4 | tablespoons sunflower seeds (ground) |
| 4 | tablespoons flaxseeds (ground) |
| 1/4 | cup fresh apple juice |

Mix together the oats and the ground ingredients, and store in the refrigerator. Soak 1/2 cup of the grain mixture with apple juice overnight in the refrigerator. Add cinnamon and 1 cup of fresh fruit; stir together.

**Exchanges per Serving:**
Fruits: 1
Grains and starches: 2
Fats: 3

**Nutritional Information per Serving:**
Calories: 350
Carbohydrate: 55%
Protein: 18%
Fat: 27%
Fiber: 1 g
Calcium: 94 mg

**Comments:** The cinnamon and fruit can also be added the night before.

••••

# ···· *Happy Apple Breakfast*

*Makes 2 Servings*

| | |
|---|---|
| 1 1/2 | cups rolled oats |
| 2 1/2 | cups water, milk, or apple juice |
| 1 | sliced medium green or golden apple |
| 1/2 | teaspoon cinnamon |
| | Milk as garnish (optional) |
| | Honey as garnish (optional) |
| 1/4 | cup currants, raisins, or chopped dates (optional) |
| 1/4 | cup fresh or roasted pumpkin seeds (optional) |

Combine all the ingredients except the garnishes, and simmer on the stove for 10 minutes. Cover and let steam for 5 more minutes. Serve with honey if extra sweetness is desired.

*Exchanges per Serving:*
Fruits: 1/2
Grains and starches: 2

*Nutritional Information per Serving:*
Calories: 184
Carbohydrate: 73%
Protein: 15%
Fat: 12%
Fiber: 2 g
Calcium: 37 mg

*Comments:* Other rolled grains such as wheat, barley, rye, or triticale can be used in various combinations, instead of some or all of the rolled oats. All of these grains have the same cooking characteristics.

◆◆◆◆

# ••••*Homestyle Baked Beans*

*Makes 4 Servings*

| | |
|---|---|
| 1 | cup dry navy, marrow, or other beans |
| 3 | cups water |
| 1 | bay leaf |
| 1 | clove garlic, minced or pressed |
| 1 | medium onion, chopped |
| 1 | tablespoon chopped parsley |
| 1/2 | cup finely diced celery |
| 1 | tablespoon vegetable oil |
| 2 | small sweet pickles, chopped |
| 1 | can (8 1/4-ounce) stewed tomatoes, mashed |
| 1/2 | teaspoon dried basil leaves, crumbled |
| 3/4 | teaspoon Lite Salt or salt substitute |
| 1/8 | teaspoon black pepper |

Wash and pick over the beans. Put them in a large saucepan with the water. Bring to a boil, and boil for 2 minutes. Cover and let stand for 1 hour. Add the bay leaf, garlic, onion, and parsley. Bring to a boil again. Cover loosely and simmer for 45 minutes or until the beans are just tender (time required will vary with kind of bean used). Drain, if necessary. Put the beans in a 1 1/2-quart casserole.

Sauté the celery in the oil for about 5 minutes. Add pickles, basil, salt, and black pepper. Bring to a boil for 10 minutes, stirring occasionally. Stir this mixture into the beans. Cover and bake at 250°F for 2 hours.

*Exchanges per Serving:*
Vegetables: 3/4          Legumes: 1 1/2     Fats: 1/2

*Nutritional Information per Serving:*
Calories: 177            Protein: 13%       Fiber: 3 g
Carbohydrate: 67%        Fat: 20%           Calcium: 71 mg

*Comments:* This is a much more healthful version of baked beans than the canned types sold commercially, which are full of saturated fats (lard).

◆◆◆◆

# ••••*Hot Cereal*

*Makes 2 Servings*

| | |
|---|---|
| 5 | **cups water** |
| 2 | **cups rolled oats** |
| 1/2 | **teaspoon vanilla extract (optional)** |
| 1/4 | **teaspoon cinnamon (optional)** |
| 4 | **tablespoons honey** |
| 1/2 | **teaspoon low-salt butter** |

Combine the water and oats in a medium-size saucepan. Cook covered over medium heat for approximately 5 minutes or until bubbling. Reduce heat and simmer uncovered for 15 minutes or until the oats are soft, stirring occasionally. Add the vanilla, honey, cinnamon, and butter. For creamier cereal, simmer for 5 minutes longer.

*Exchanges per Serving:*
Fruits: 1/2     Grains and starches: 1     Fats: 1/2

*Nutritional Information per Serving:*
Calories: 140          Protein: 14%          Fiber: 1.6 g
Carbohydrate: 70%     Fat: 16%              Calcium: 31 mg

*Comments:* Instead of using honey, you can add one sliced banana, 1/2 cup of raisins, or 1/2 cup fruit juice during the last few minutes of cooking.

◆◆◆◆

# ••••*Indian Rice with Peas and Pepper*

*Makes 8 Servings*

| | |
|---|---|
| 1 | teaspoon olive oil |
| 2 | cloves garlic |
| 1 | medium onion |
| 1 1/2 | teaspoons curry |
| 4 | cups water |
| 3/4 | teaspoon Lite Salt or salt substitute |
| 2 | cups basmati or brown rice |
| 1 | cup cooked green peas |
| 1 | cup diced sweet red pepper |

In a large saucepan or dutch oven, heat the oil briefly, add the garlic and onion, and sauté the vegetables for a few minutes. Stir in the curry powder, and sauté the vegetables 1 minute longer. Then add the water and salt, and bring the ingredients to a boil. Stir in the rice, reduce the heat to low, cover the pan, and simmer the rice for 40 minutes or until the water is almost completely absorbed. Add the peas and red pepper, and cook the rice for 5 minutes longer.

*Exchanges per Serving:*
Vegetables: 1/8                    Legumes: 1/2
Grains and starches: 1/2          Fats: 1/8

*Nutritional Information per Serving:*
Calories: 90              Protein: 9%          Fiber: 2g
Carbohydrate: 71%         Fat: 20%             Calcium: 18 mg

*Comments:* This is the classic accompaniment to a spicy Indian main dish.

◆ ◆ ◆

# ••••*Pinto Beans and Corn*

*Makes 4 Servings*

| | |
|---|---|
| 1 | tablespoon virgin olive oil |
| 1 | onion, chopped |
| 1 | red bell pepper, diced |
| 2 | cups homemade vegetable stock |
| 1 | cup chopped tomato |
| 1 | cup corn, fresh or frozen |
| 4 | cups cooked (or canned) pinto beans |
| 1/2 | teaspoon chili powder |
| 1/4 | teaspoon cumin powder |
| 1 | teaspoon dried oregano |

Cook 2 cups of pinto beans according to the guidelines in Table 8.1, and set aside. In a large pot, sauté the onion and red pepper in the oil until tender. Add the stock, tomato, and corn. Mash two cups of pinto beans, and add these to the pot along with two cups of whole beans. Add the seasonings. Simmer for 40 minutes.

*Exchanges per Serving:*
Vegetables: 1/2            Legumes: 2
Grains and starches: 1     Fats: 1/2

*Nutritional Information per Serving:*
Calories: 256          Protein: 15%        Fiber: 4 g
Carbohydrate: 64%      Fat: 21%            Calcium: 52 mg

**Comments:** This simple recipe is easy to prepare and is highly nutritious.

••••

# •••• *Refried Beans*

*Makes 6 Servings*

| | |
|---|---|
| 1 | pound dried pinto beans, picked over, rinsed, and soaked 10 hours or longer in water to cover (by at least 4 inches) |
| | Water to cover by 2 inches |
| 2 | large cloves garlic, peeled and divided |
| 1 | medium onion, peeled |
| 1 | teaspoon Lite Salt or salt substitute, divided |
| 2 | teaspoons olive oil or canola oil |
| 1/2 | cup minced onion (1 small) |
| 2 | dashes hot pepper sauce or cayenne, or to taste |

Drain the beans, rinse them, and place them in a large sauce-pan with water to cover by at least 2 inches. Add 1 garlic clove and the peeled whole onion. Bring the liquid to a boil, reduce the heat, partially cover the pan, and simmer the beans for 40 minutes. Add 1/2 teaspoon of the salt, and cook the beans for 20 minutes longer or until the beans are tender. Drain the beans, reserving the cooking liquid. Discard the garlic and onion. Transfer the beans to a bowl with a flat bottom, and mash them lightly, leaving lots of whole or partially mashed beans.

Mince the remaining clove of garlic. In a small skillet, heat the oil briefly, add the minced garlic and minced onion, and sauté the ingredients for several minutes or until the onion turns golden. Add the onion mixture to the beans, along with the hot pepper sauce or cayenne and the remaining 1/2 teaspoon of salt. Stir the mixture to combine the ingredients well.

*Exchanges per Serving:*
Legumes: 1                              Fats: 1/3

*Nutritional Information per Serving:*
Calories: 100 g
Carbohydrate: 68%
Protein: 23%
Fat: 9%
Fiber: 6 g
Calcium: 32 mg

*Comments:* This dish can be made ahead and reheated in the oven or microwave at serving time. Canned refried beans are typically prepared using lard, and even the vegetarian versions are usually very high in fats.

◆◆◆◆

# ••••*Skillet Bulgur and Vegetables with Shredded Basil*

*Makes 4 Servings*

2   cups bulgur wheat
1   tablespoon vegetable oil
2   cloves garlic, mined
2   medium onions, diced
2   small to medium zucchini (sliced)
1   tablespoon basil
2   medium carrots, grated
2   teaspoons tamari soy sauce
    Dash of Lite Salt or salt substitute
    Ground pepper

Rinse the bulgur in a sieve under cold running water. Place in a medium-size bowl, and pour enough boiling water over it to cover it. Let soak for 30 minutes. Transfer small batches at a time to a large piece of cheesecloth or a clean kitchen towel, and squeeze out all the liquid. Place the bulgur in a bowl, and set it aside.

In a large skillet, heat the oil over medium-high heat until it is hot. Add the garlic and onions, and sauté for 5 minutes. Add the zucchini and basil, and cook for 5 minutes, tossing occasionally. Add the carrots and cook for a few more minutes. Add the bulgur, soy sauce, Lite Salt or salt substitute, and pepper; and cook for 2 to 3 minutes or until the bulgur is hot.

*Exchanges per Serving:*
Vegetables: 1
Grains and starches: 1
Fats: 3/4

*Nutritional Information per Serving:*
Calories: 341
Carbohydrates: 67%
Protein: 11%
Fat: 22%
Fiber: 8 g
Calcium: 74 mg

*Comments:* The key to this recipe is the fresh basil.

◆◆◆

# ••••*Tabouli*

*Makes 6 Servings*

| | |
|---|---|
| 1 | cup bulgur wheat |
| 2 | cups water |
| 2 | tomatoes, finely diced |
| 1 | bunch scallions with tops, finely chopped |
| 1 | cup finely chopped fresh parsley |
| 3 | tablespoons chopped fresh mint leaves or 2 teaspoons dried mint |
| 1/4 | cup fresh lemon juice |
| 2 | tablespoons virgin olive oil |
| 1/4 | teaspoon black pepper |
| 1/4 | teaspoon dried oregano |
| 1/4 | teaspoon ground cumin |
| 1/4 | teaspoon allspice |
| 1/4 | teaspoon coriander |

Bring the water to a boil. Pour into a medium-size bowl, and soak the bulgur for 1 hour. Drain the bulgur well, pressing out the excess water through a fine strainer or cheesecloth. Add the tomatoes, scallions, parsley, and mint to the bulgur. Combine the ingredients well. Set aside. In a small bowl, combine the lemon juice, oil, pepper, oregano, cumin, allspice, and coriander. Add this to the bulgur mixture, and toss to coat well. Marinate for 1 hour before serving.

*Exchanges per Serving:*
| | |
|---|---|
| Vegetables: 1/2 | Grains and starches: 1 |
| Fruits: 1/6 | Fats: 1 |

*Nutritional Information per Serving:*
| | | |
|---|---|---|
| Calories: 162 | Protein: 8% | Fiber: trace |
| Carbohydrate: 65% | Fat: 27% | Calcium: 38 mg |

*Comments:* Tabouli provides excellent nutrition, especially since the vegetables, herbs, and spices are not exposed to heat.

◆◆◆◆

## ◆◆◆◆ *Wild Rice with Mushrooms*

*Makes 4 Servings*

| | |
|---|---|
| 1 1/3 | cups uncooked wild rice |
| 4 | cups boiling water |
| 1/4 | cup olive oil |
| 2 | tablespoons finely chopped scallion |
| 2 | tablespoons minced parsley |
| 2 | tablespoons minced chives |
| 2 | tablespoons minced green pepper |
| 1 | pound mushrooms |
| 1 | teaspoon Lite Salt or salt substitute |
| 1 | teaspoon black pepper |

Cook the rice in the water for 45 minutes. Then sauté the onion, parsley, chives, and green pepper in the olive oil for about 3 minutes. Add the whole mushrooms, and cook for another 5 minutes. Combine the wild rice and cooked vegetables, and season with salt and black pepper.

*Exchanges per Serving:*
Vegetables: 3/4    Grains and starches: 1/2    Fats: 2

*Nutritional Information per Serving:*
Calories: 130          Protein: 20%          Fiber: 5 g
Carbohydrate: 50%     Fat: 30%              Calcium: 14 mg

*Comments:* Although any mushroom will do, the standard button mushroom works best.

◆◆◆◆

# 9

## ••••Vegetarian Entrées

Given the expanding population of the world, there is a growing need to meet human nutritional needs in the most economical and environmentally sound way possible. Grains and legumes are viewed as offering the greatest promise. The two foods work well together in many respects. For example, the amino acid patterns complement each other in such a way that the shortcomings of one are supplied by the other. Specifically, the low lysine content of grains is compensated for by the high lysine content of legumes, while the low methionine and cysteine content of many legumes is compensated for by the higher methionine and cysteine content of grains. Furthermore, certain legumes (including soybeans) convert nitrogen gas from the air into soil ("fixed") nitrogen. The soil is then more suitable for growing grains. After the grains have depleted the nitrogen, these legumes can again be planted to renourish the soil with nitrogen.

The entrée recipes given in this chapter provide excellent protein content and amino acid profiles. They are also high in fiber. Since a vegetarian diet has been suggested as the role model to help Americans reduce their risk for heart disease, cancer, and strokes, these recipes and other vegetarian dishes must replace meat-based main dishes.

# ••••*Baked Eggplant, Chick-peas, and Tomatoes*

*Makes 4 Servings*

1   large eggplant, peeled and cut into chunks
1   tablespoon vegetable oil
2   medium onions, diced
3   cloves garlic, minced
1   pound fresh tomatoes (chopped)
2   cups cooked chick-peas
    Ground pepper
1/2 cup parsley

Preheat oven to 350°F. Heat the oil in a large skillet. Add the eggplant, simmering and tossing regularly until it is browned and tender. Remove the eggplant from the pan, and sauté the onions. Add the tomatoes and cook for 5 minutes. Add the chick-peas and eggplant, and toss well. Season with Lite Salt or salt substitute and pepper, and cook for 5 more minutes. Transfer to a medium-size baking dish, and bake for 20 minutes or until hot and bubbly.

*Exchanges per Serving:*
Vegetables: 1          Legumes: 1          Fats: 3/4

*Nutritional Information per Serving:*
Calories: 196          Protein: 14%          Fiber: 9 g
Carbohydrate: 56%      Fat: 30%              Calcium: 93 mg

*Comments:* This dish should be served with a brown rice dish such as Country-style Rice.

◆◆◆◆

# ···· *Bean Burritos*

*Makes 4 Servings*

|     |                                                       |
|-----|-------------------------------------------------------|
| 2   | cups cooked red kidney beans                          |
| 1   | teaspoon canola oil                                   |
| 1/2 | cup chopped onion                                     |
| 1/4 | cup diced red or green bell pepper                    |
| 1   | clove garlic, minced                                  |
| 3/4 | teaspoon ground cumin                                 |
| 1/2 | teaspoon ground coriander                             |
| 1/8 | teaspoon white pepper                                 |
| 1/2 | cup frozen whole kernel corn, thawed and drained      |
| 4   | (8-inch) flour tortillas                              |
| 3/4 | cup (3 ounces) soy cheese                             |
| 1   | cup medium salsa                                      |

Place the cooked kidney beans in a medium-size bowl, and mash these to the desired consistency. Coat a small nonstick skillet with canola oil, and place it over medium heat until hot. Add the onion, red bell pepper, and garlic; and sauté for 5 minutes or until the onion is tender. Stir in the cumin, coriander, and white pepper. Cook for 1 minute, and remove from heat. Add the onion mixture and corn to the beans; stir well.

Divide the bean mixture evenly among the tortillas, spreading it to the edges. Sprinkle the soy cheese down the center of each tortilla. Roll up; place, seam side down, on a baking sheet. Bake at 425°F for 5 minutes or until thoroughly heated. Spoon salsa over the burritos. Serve warm.

**Exchanges per Serving:**
Vegetables: 1 1/4          Legumes: 1 1/4
Grains and starches: 1 1/4     Fats: 1

*Nutritional Information per Serving:*
Calories: 295
Carbohydrate: 61%
Protein: 22%
Fat: 17%
Fiber: 11 g
Calcium: 231 mg

*Comments:* This dish can serve as the entrée for a Mexican fiesta.

◆ ◆ ◆ ◆

# ◆◆◆◆*Bean Tostadas*

*Makes 4 Servings*

| | |
|---|---|
| 5 | tablespoons olive oil |
| 1 | clove garlic, minced |
| 1 | medium onion, diced |
| 2 | cups cooked kidney beans or black beans |
| 1/2 | cup water |
| 4 | (6-inch) flour tortillas |
| 2 | cups grated soy cheese |
| | Salsa |

Heat 2 tablespoons of the oil in a large skillet over medium heat. Add the garlic and onions, and sauté until the onions are tender (about 10 minutes). Add the beans and water, and simmer for 5 minutes. Mash half of the beans with the back of a spoon, and stir to mix. Keep warm over low heat while preparing the tortillas.

Set oven on broil. Brush the tortillas on both sides with the 3 remaining tablespoons of oil, lay them on a cookie sheet, and broil them on both sides until crisp. Divide the beans equally, and spread them on each tortilla. Top with equal amounts of grated soy cheese. Return to the broiler, and broil until the cheese is melted and bubbly. Serve immediately, topped with salsa.

*Exchanges per Serving:*
Vegetables: 1/4
Grains and starches: 1
Legumes: 1 1/2
Fats: 3/4

*Nutritional Information per Serving:*
Calories: 260
Carbohydrate: 55%
Protein: 22%
Fat: 23%
Fiber: 10 g
Calcium: 334 mg

*Comments:* If regular cheese is preferred, choose a low-fat variety.

◆◆◆◆

# ◆◆◆◆ *Braised Tempeh Napoletano*

*Makes 4 Servings*

|       |                                                           |
|-------|-----------------------------------------------------------|
| 1     | tablespoon olive oil                                      |
| 5     | cloves garlic, minced                                     |
| 1     | medium onion                                              |
| 2     | small zucchini, halved lengthwise and thinly sliced       |
| 1     | large green pepper (diced)                                |
| 8     | ounces tempeh (cut into 1/2-inch cubes)                   |
| 1 1/2 | cups finely chopped peeled tomatoes, with their juice     |
| 1/2   | teaspoon basil                                            |
| 1/2   | teaspoon marjoram                                         |
| 1/2   | teaspoon Lite Salt or salt substitute                     |
|       | Fresh ground pepper                                       |

Heat the olive oil in a large skillet over medium-high heat; then add the garlic and onion, and sauté for 2 minutes, tossing frequently. Add the green pepper and tempeh, and cook, tossing occasionally. Add the tomatoes and all of the remaining ingredients, and stir well. Reduce the heat to a simmer, and cook slowly for about 10 minutes, or until the sauce is fragrant and thickened. Do not overcook the vegetables; they should retain a slight crunchiness. Serve immediately.

*Exchanges per Serving:*
Vegetables: 3/4         Legumes: 1/2         Fats: 1 1/2

*Nutritional Information per Serving:*
Calories: 256         Protein: 10%         Fiber: 3 g
Carbohydrate: 60%    Fat: 30%             Calcium: 58 mg

*Comments:* Most tempeh dishes are Asian; this one is a pleasant change of pace if you like tempeh.

◆◆◆◆

# •••• *Corn and Kidney Bean Pie*

*Makes 6 Servings*

|       |                                          |
|-------|------------------------------------------|
| 2     | cups yellow cornmeal                     |
| 2     | tablespoons safflower oil                |
| 3/4   | cup vegetable stock                      |
| 1     | onion, chopped                           |
| 1/2   | cup chopped carrot                       |
| 1/2   | cup chopped celery                       |
| 1/2   | cup water                                |
| 1     | cup dry (or 16-ounce can) kidney beans   |
|       | Cayenne pepper to taste                  |
| 1     | teaspoon ground cumin                    |
| 2     | tablespoons low-sodium soy sauce         |
| 1/3   | cup grated sharp soy cheese              |

To make the crust, combine the cornmeal, oil, and 1/2 cup of heated stock; and pat into a lightly oiled, deep 9-inch pie or cake dish. Cook the beans according to the guidelines in Table 8.1 (page 145), or use a 16-ounce can of kidney beans. After cooking (or draining, if using canned beans), pour the soy sauce over the beans. Briefly cook the onion, carrot, and celery in the vegetable stock or water. Mix the spices and vegetables with the beans, and turn the mixture into the cornmeal crust. Bake at 350°F for approximately 25 minutes. Remove from oven, sprinkle with soy cheese, and bake for 5 minutes more.

*Exchanges per Serving:*
Vegetables: 1/3
Grains and starches: 2 1/2
Legumes: 1/3
Fats: 1

*Nutritional Information per Serving:*
Calories: 280          Protein: 12%          Fiber: 1 g
Carbohydrate: 64%          Fat: 24%          Calcium: 66 mg

*Comments:* This recipe provides a high-quality protein due to the near perfect complementary amino acid profiles of the corn and kidney beans.

◆◆◆◆

# ◆◆◆◆*Eggplant Curry*

*Makes 4 Servings*

| | |
|---|---|
| 1 | pound eggplant (approximately 4 cups), peeled and cut into 1-inch cubes |
| 1 | tablespoon olive oil |
| 2 | tablespoons curry powder |
| 1 | teaspoon ground cumin |
| 2 | large cloves garlic, finely minced |
| | Black pepper to taste |
| 1/2 | cup homemade vegetable stock |
| 1 | medium carrot, thinly sliced |
| 1 | cup diced potatoes |
| 1 | green bell pepper, thinly sliced |
| 1 | large onion, thinly sliced |
| 1 | cup bite-size cauliflower florets |
| 1 | cup peeled, seeded, and chopped tomatoes (do not drain) |
| 1/4 | cup low-sodium tomato juice |
| 1 | cup cooked chick-peas |

In a large skillet, heat 1 tablespoon of the oil. Add the eggplant. Cook, stirring often, for approximately 5 minutes. Remove the eggplant from the pan and set aside. Heat the oil remaining in the skillet, and add the curry, cumin, garlic, and pepper. Stir in the vegetable stock, and cook the mixture for 2 minutes. Add the carrots, potatoes, green pepper, onions, and cauliflower. Simmer, covered, for 5 to 7 minutes or until the vegetables are tender-crisp. Return the eggplant to the pan, and add the tomatoes (with their juice) and chick-peas. Simmer the curry, covered, for 10 minutes more before serving.

*Exchanges per Serving:*
Vegetables: 2 1/2
Grains and starches: 1/4
Legumes: 1/4
Fats: 3/4

*Nutritional Information per Serving:*
Calories: 263
Carbohydrate: 65%
Protein: 14%
Fat: 21%
Fiber: 4 g
Calcium: 191 mg

*Comments:* This dish goes extremely well with Indian Rice.

◆ ◆ ◆

# ••••*Gingered Tempeh and Vegetables*

*Makes 4 Servings*

| | |
|---|---|
| 2 | cups brown rice |
| 1/2 | teaspoon canola oil |
| | 8-ounce package tempeh, quartered and cut diagonally to make 8 triangles |
| 2 | teaspoons fresh ginger juice* |
| 2 | tablespoons low-sodium soy sauce |
| 2 | teaspoons dry mustard |
| 3 | cups plus 2 tablespoons cold water |
| 2 | teaspoons sesame oil |
| 2 | carrots, thinly sliced |
| 2 | parsnips, thinly sliced |
| 2 | cups thinly sliced broccoli |
| 4 | stalks celery, thinly sliced |
| 2 | cups chopped bok choy |
| 1 | cup mung bean sprouts |
| 1 | tablespoon arrowroot |

Cook the rice according to the guidelines in Table 8.1 (page 145). Place the tempeh in a lightly oiled baking dish. In a small bowl, combine the ginger juice, soy sauce, mustard, and 2 tablespoons of water; and pour this over the tempeh. Bake for 15 minutes at 350°F. Turn and bake for 10 minutes more. Meanwhile, warm the sesame oil in the skillet. Sauté the carrots and parsnips, stirring over medium heat for a few minutes. Add 2 cups of water, quickly cover, and simmer for 5 minutes. Add the broccoli, celery, bok choy, and bean sprouts. Simmer, covered, for 3 to 5 minutes, until just crunchy. Dissolve the arrowroot in the remaining water, and stir this into the vegetables until the sauce thickens. Transfer to a serving dish.

*Exchanges per Serving:*

| | |
|---|---|
| Vegetables: 3 | Legumes: 2 |
| Grains and starches: 1 | Fats: 1 1/4 |

*Nutritional Information per Serving:*

| | | |
|---|---|---|
| Calories: 468 | Protein: 20% | Fiber: 8 g |
| Carbohydrate: 59% | Fat: 21% | Calcium: 337 mg |

*Comments:* This dish has it all: vegetables, whole grain, and legumes.

*To make ginger juice, fine-grate the ginger, and squeeze it in your fingers over a bowl.

◆◆◆◆

# ••••*Indonesian Curried Vegetable Stew with Coconut Milk*

*Makes 4 Servings*

| | |
|---|---|
| 1 | tablespoon olive oil |
| 2 | medium onion |
| 1/8 | teaspoon cayenne pepper |
| 4 | cloves garlic, minced |
| 1 | tablespoon minced ginger root |
| 1 | tablespoon ground coriander |
| 1 | teaspoon ground cumin |
| 1 | teaspoon turmeric |
| | Ground black pepper |
| | Grated rind of 1 lemon |
| 1 1/2 | cups sliced mushrooms |
| 3 | cups vegetable stock |
| 1 1/2 | cups coconut milk |
| 2 | large potatoes, peeled and diced |
| 1 1/2 | cups vermicelli noodles |
| 2 | cups broccoli florets |
| | Juice of 1 lemon |
| 4 | lemon wedges |

Have all of the ingredients in front of you before you begin. In a medium-size saucepan, heat the oil and add the onions and cayenne. Sauté for 5 minutes or until the onions begin to turn golden. Add the garlic and ginger root, stir, and then add all of the spices and the lemon rind. Cook for 3 minutes. Add the mushrooms and cook for 5 minutes; then add the vegetable stock, coconut milk, and Lite Salt or salt substitute. Bring the contents to a boil, and add the potatoes. Cook uncovered for about 10 minutes, stirring occasionally or until the potatoes are almost tender. Add the noodles and let the mixture return to a boil. Then add the broccoli. Cook, stirring frequently, for about 5 minutes or until the noodles are tender. Add the lemon juice and stir to blend. Serve in bowls, with lemon wedges on the side.

*Exchanges per Serving:*
Vegetables: 1 1/2
Fruits: 1/4
Grains and starches: 1 1/4
Fats: 1 1/4

*Nutritional Information per Serving:*
Calories: 250
Carbohydrate: 65%
Protein: 12%
Fat: 23%
Fiber: 6.5 g
Calcium: 104 mg

*Comments:* If you are looking for a main course soup or stew, this is a fantastic choice.

◆ ◆ ◆

# ⬩⬩⬩⬩ *Mexican Polenta Pie*

*Makes 4 Servings*

| | |
|---|---|
| 2 | tablespoons safflower oil |
| 1 | small onion, coarsely chopped |
| 8 | ounces mushrooms, thinly sliced |
| 1 | teaspoon cumin seeds |
| 1 | teaspoon chili powder |
| 1/4 | teaspoon crushed red pepper |
| 2 | cups cooked black beans |
| | 28-ounce can plum tomatoes (28 ounces) drained |
| | 4-ounce can chopped mild green chilies, drained |
| 3/4 | teaspoon Lite Salt or salt substitute |
| 2/3 | cup instant polenta* |
| 1/2 | cup soy cheese |

Follow the guidelines in Table 8.1 (page 145) for cooking the black beans; or if you are in a hurry, use two drained 16-ounce cans of black beans. Preheat the oven to 400°F. In a large skillet, heat the oil over moderately high heat. Add the onion and cook, stirring occasionally, until it is slightly softened (about 3 minutes). Add the mushrooms, cumin seeds, chili powder, and crushed red pepper. Cook, stirring occasionally, until the mushrooms soften and release their juices (about 3 minutes). Crush the tomatoes and add them to the skillet. Stir in the green chilies and black beans. Reduce the heat to moderate, and simmer for at least 10 minutes. Stir in 1/4 teaspoon of the Lite Salt or salt substitute.

Meanwhile, in a 10-inch (preferably cast-iron) skillet, combine 2 cups of water and the remaining 1/2 teaspoon Lite Salt or salt substitute. Bring to a boil over high heat, and stir in the polenta. Reduce the heat to moderately high and cook, stirring, until the polenta holds its shape (about 5 minutes). Remove from the heat, and spread the polenta evenly in the skillet. If you do not have a cast-iron skillet, spread the polenta in a pie pan. Set aside for 5 minutes.

Spread the black bean mixture evenly over the polenta. Sprinkle the soy cheese on top. Bake for 12 to 15 minutes, until the chili is bubbling and the cheese is melted. Let stand for 15 minutes before serving.

*Exchanges per Serving:*
Vegetables: 1
Grains and starches: 1 1/2
Legumes: 1 1/8
Fats: 1 1/2

*Nutritional Information per Serving:*
Calories: 306
Carbohydrate: 50%
Protein: 21%
Fat: 29%
Fiber: 12 g
Calcium: 310 mg

*Comments:* If you cook the beans ahead of time or use canned beans, this is a quick and easy recipe.

*Available at most food stores and all specialty food stores.

◆ ◆ ◆

# ••••*Mushroom Stroganoff with Tofu*

*Makes 4 Servings*

*Sauce*

| | |
|---|---|
| 8 | ounces tofu |
| 1/4 | cup water |
| 2 | tablespoons soy sauce |
| 2 | tablespoons lemon juice or cider vinegar |
| 1 | clove garlic |
| 1 | teaspoon chopped ginger root |

*Stroganoff*

| | |
|---|---|
| 1/2 | onion, minced |
| 1 | clove garlic, minced (optional) |
| 1 | teaspoon canola oil or olive oil |
| 1 | pound fresh mushrooms, sliced |
| 4 | ounces tofu |
| 1 | teaspoon oregano |
| 1 | tablespoon toasted slivered almonds |
| 1 | tablespoon chopped fresh parsley |
| 2 | cups cooked brown rice |

Make the sauce first, by combining and blending all the sauce ingredients in a blender. Blend until very smooth. Make sure that the garlic, lemon rind, and ginger root are finely chopped and not left in big chunks. Set aside or refrigerate to use later; this improves the flavor. The sauce will keep for up to 1 week.

To make the stroganoff, sauté the onion and garlic in oil until the onion is translucent. Add the mushrooms and sauté until these are slightly limp and their moisture has evaporated. Set aside. Cut the tofu into 1-inch cubes, and brown these slightly.

Pour the sauce over all. Mix well and heat through, stirring. Blend in the oregano. Serve over cooked brown rice (1/2 cup per person), and sprinkle with toasted almonds and parsley.

*Exchanges per Serving:*
Vegetables: 1/2                    Legumes: 1
Grains and starches: 1             Fats: 1/2

*Nutritional Information per Serving:*
Calories: 208          Protein: 21%        Fiber: 3 g
Carbohydrate: 56%      Fat: 23%            Calcium: 160 mg

*Comments:* This is a great alternative to Beef Stroganoff.

◆ ◆ ◆ ◆

# ◆◆◆◆ *Polenta Puttanesca*

*Makes 4 Servings*

*Sauce*

| | |
|---|---|
| 1 | tablespoon olive oil |
| 7 | cloves garlic |
| 1/4 | teaspoon dried red pepper flakes |
| 2 | large green peppers, cut into strips |
| 2 | pounds of tomatoes, chopped and drained |
| 2 | tablespoons tomato paste |
| 6 | black olives, halved |
| 2 | teaspoons capers |
| 1/4 | teaspoon Lite Salt or salt substitute |
| | Ground pepper, to taste |

*Polenta*

| | |
|---|---|
| **4** | **cups water** |
| **1 1/4** | **cups cornmeal** |
| **1/3** | **teaspoon Lite Salt or salt substitute** |
| **1/3** | **cup grated soy cheese** |

In a large skillet, heat the oil over medium heat until hot. Then add the garlic and red pepper flakes, and cook for 3 minutes. Add the green peppers, and sauté for 10 minutes. Add the tomatoes, tomato paste, olives, capers, Lite Salt or salt substitute, and pepper. Cook until the peppers are tender and the sauce thickens.

Meanwhile make the polenta. In a medium-size saucepan, bring the water to a boil. Drizzle in the polenta slowly, whisking continuously with a wire whisk. Add the Lite Salt or salt substitute, and reduce the heat to low. Continue to whisk the polenta until it forms a thick mass. Stir continuously until the polenta pulls away from the sides of the pan (5 to 7 minutes)

To serve, spoon equal portions of the polenta onto the center of each serving plate. Top with the sauce and serve immediately.

**Exchanges per Serving:**
Vegetables: 1 1/2
Grains and starches: 2
Fats: 1
Milk: 1/8

**Nutritional Information per Serving:**

| | | |
|---|---|---|
| Calories: 254 | Protein: 9% | Fiber: 3 g |
| Carbohydrate: 61% | Fat: 30% | Calcium: 192 mg |

**Comments:** Instead of adding tomatoes and tomato paste, you can add 16 ounces of all-natural spaghetti sauce.

◆◆◆◆

# ••••*Rice with Beans and Vegetables*

*Makes 4 Servings*

| | |
|---|---|
| 1 | cup cooked long-grain brown rice |
| 1/4 | cup water |
| 1 | medium onion, coarsely chopped |
| 2 | cloves garlic, finely minced |
| 2 | medium tomatoes, finely diced |
| 1 | medium zucchini, coarsely chopped |
| 1/2 | teaspoon dried oregano |
| 2 | cups cooked or canned beans (kidney, pink, black, or garbanzo) |
| | Black pepper to taste |

Cook the rice and beans according to the guidelines in Table 8.1 (page 145). Meanwhile, heat the water in a large skillet, and add the onion and garlic. Cook these until tender. Add the tomatoes, zucchini, and oregano. Simmer, covered, for 5 minutes or until the vegetables are tender-crisp. Add the beans and simmer, stirring occasionally, until heated through. Season with pepper. To serve, spoon the mixture over the rice.

*Exchanges per Serving:*
Vegetables: 1     Grains and starches: 1/2   Legumes: 1

*Nutritional Information per Serving:*
Calories: 190          Protein: 15%        Fiber: 2 g
Carbohydrate: 80%      Fat: 5%             Calcium: 77 mg

*Comments:* Other vegetables such as carrots, celery, and potatoes can be added if desired.

◆ ◆ ◆ ◆

# ••••*Soybean Casserole*

*Makes 6 Servings*

| | |
|---|---|
| 1 | **cup soybeans** |
| 2 1/2 | **cups brown rice** |
| 2 | **cups corn, fresh or frozen** |
| 2 | **cups canned low-sodium tomatoes** |
| 1 | **cup chopped onion** |
| 1/2 | **cup chopped celery** |
| 1 | **clove garlic, crushed** |
| 1/2 | **teaspoon thyme** |
| 1/2 | **teaspoon savory** |
| | **Cayenne pepper to taste** |
| 1/4 | **cup low-sodium tomato paste** |
| 1/2 | **cup homemade vegetable stock** |
| 1/2 | **teaspoon olive oil** |
| 1/2 | **cup grated soy cheese** |

Cook soybeans and rice separately, according to the guidelines in Table 8.1 (page 145). In a medium-size bowl, combine the soybeans, corn, tomatoes, onion, celery, garlic, herbs, and spices. In a small bowl, combine the tomato paste and stock. Place half of the cooked rice in a lightly oiled large casserole dish, and cover with the vegetable mixture. Spread the tomato paste over the vegetables and cover this with the remaining rice. Sprinkle with grated soy cheese. Bake, uncovered, for 30 minutes at 350°F.

**Exchanges per Serving:**

| | |
|---|---|
| Vegetables: 1 | Legumes: 2 1/6 |
| Grains and starches: 2 | Fats: 1/4 |

**Nutritional Information per Serving:**

| | | |
|---|---|---|
| Calories: 369 | Protein: 14% | Fiber: 3 g |
| Carbohydrate: 76% | Fat: 10% | Calcium: 148 mg |

*Comments:* This highly nutritious casserole has it all: excellent protein quality, healthful vegetables, and numerous medicinal herbs and spices, including garlic.

♦♦♦♦

# ••••*Spicy Bulgur with Red Beans*

*Makes 4 Servings*

| | |
|---|---|
| 1 1/4 | cups bulgur wheat |
| 1 | tablespoon virgin olive oil |
| 1/2 | cup chopped green onion |
| 1/2 | green bell pepper, diced |
| 2 | cups water |
| 2 | large tomatoes, chopped |
| 1 | cup cooked red beans |
| 1 | clove garlic, minced |
| 1/8 | teaspoon black pepper |
| 1 | teaspoon paprika |
| | Cayenne pepper to taste |

Cook the red beans the night before, according to the guidelines in Table 8.1 (page 145). Sauté the bulgur in the oil until golden. Add the remaining ingredients, including the cooked red beans. Cover and bring to a boil. Reduce heat and simmer for 15 minutes, adding more hot water if necessary.

*Exchanges per Serving:*
Vegetables: 1/2
Grains and starches: 2
Legumes: 1/2
Fats: 3/4

*Nutritional Information per Serving:*
Calories: 259          Protein: 12%          Fiber: 1 g
Carbohydrate: 75%      Fat: 13%              Calcium: 29 mg

*Comments:* An excellent whole-grain and legume recipe.

◆◆◆◆

# ◆◆◆◆ *Stir-fried Noodles and Vegetables with Sesame Seeds*

*Makes 4 Servings*

|     | 8-ounce package of Chinese noodles |
| 2   | cups broccoli florets |
| 1/4 | cup chopped ginger root |
| 6   | ounces firm tofu, cut into 1/2-inch cubes |
| 2   | large onions, quartered and sliced |
| 2   | cloves garlic, minced |
| 1   | tablespoon tamari soy sauce |
| 2   | tablespoons sesame seeds |
| 1   | teaspoon Oriental sesame oil |

First, cook the noodles in boiling water, drain them in a collander, and pour cold water over them in the sink. Set the cooled noodles aside.

In a covered wok or large skillet, precook the broccoli over medium heat, with 1/4 cup water. Cook until tender yet still bright green (about 3 minutes). Remove the broccoli and set it aside. Drain all of the water out of the wok, and heat the wok over medium heat. Add the oil; and when this is hot, add the ginger. Cook for 5 minutes or until golden. Add the tofu to the hot oil, and stir-fry until golden. Add the onion and garlic, and stir-fry for 5 minutes or until the onions begin to get tender yet are still crunchy. Add the cooked broccoli, and toss in the wok for 1 minute. Add the noodles and toss well. Add the soy sauce and stir-fry for 2 more minutes, or until the noodles are hot. Sprinkle on the sesame seeds and sesame oil. Serve immediately.

*Exchanges per Serving:*
Vegetables: 2
Grains and starches: 1
Legumes: 1/2
Fats: 3/4

*Nutritional Information per Serving:*
Calories: 268
Carbohydrate: 61%
Protein: 20%
Fat: 19%
Fiber: 2.2 g
Calcium: 111 mg

*Comments:* This stir-fry is a good example of how tofu absorbs and retains the flavors of the foods it is cooked with.

◆ ◆ ◆ ◆

# ◆◆◆◆ *Stuffed Peppers*

*Makes 6 Servings*

|   |   |
|---|---|
| 1 | tablespoon olive oil |
| 1 | small onion, chopped |
| 1 | clove garlic, chopped |
| 12 | ounces tofu, squeezed and mashed |
| 2 | cups cooked wild rice |
| 1 | tablespoon oregano |
| 1/2 | teaspoon basil |
|   | Salt and pepper to taste |
| 6 | large red or green peppers |

Heat the olive oil and sauté the onions and garlic until they are translucent. Add the crumbled tofu, wild rice, oregano, and basil. Cook these ingredients for 5 minutes, stirring constantly to avoid burning the onions. Add Lite Salt or salt substitute and pepper, and set aside to cool slightly.

Cut off the bottoms of the peppers, remove the seeds, and wash the peppers. Fill the peppers with the tofu mixture, and steam for 10 to 15 minutes or until the stuffing is heated through. Remove the peppers from the steam, cut into wedges, and arrange nicely on a plate. Serve with a tomato or miso sauce.

*Exchanges per Serving:*
Vegetables: 1/2
Grains and starches: 1/2
Legumes: 1/2
Fats: 1/2

*Nutritional Information per Serving:*
Calories: 120
Carbohydrate: 45%
Protein: 26%
Fat: 29%
Fiber: 3 g
Calcium: 138 mg

*Comments:* This extremely appealing main dish is high in nutrition and low in calories.

◆◆◆◆

# •••• *Teriyaki Tofu*

*Makes 2 Servings*

*Tofu Base*
| | |
|---|---|
| 16 | **ounces tofu** |
| 1 | **teaspoon canola oil** |

*Teriyaki Sauce*
| | |
|---|---|
| 1/2 | **cup soy sauce** |
| 3/4 | **cup water** |
| 1/2 | **tablespoon honey** |
| 1 | **teaspoon powdered ginger, ground** |
| 1/4 | **teaspoon garlic powder** |
| 1 | **teaspoon dark sesame oil** |

Slice the tofu into pieces 2 × 2 3/4 × 1/2 inch thick. Press the
tofu slices between a double layer of dish toweling topped
with a 3-pound board for 3 minutes. Arrange the slices in a
shallow baking pan. Mix the ingredients for the teriyaki
sauce. Pour the sauce on the tofu slices, and marinate for
1 1/2 hours on each side. Drain briefly on paper towels. Heat
the canola oil in a large skillet. Add the tofu slices, and fry for
2 1/2 to 3 minutes on each side or until golden brown.

**Exchanges per Serving:**
Fruits: 1/4              Legumes: 1 1/2     Fats: 1

**Nutritional Information per Serving:**
Calories: 200           Protein: 34%        Fiber: 4 g
Carbohydrate: 40%       Fat: 26%            Calcium: 275 mg

**Comments:** This makes a great sandwich filler.

◆◆◆◆

# •••• *Tofu Burgers*

*Makes 8 Servings*

| | |
|---|---|
| **24** | **ounces tofu** |
| **8** | **tablespoons grated carrots** |
| **4** | **tablespoons minced leeks, scallions, or onion** |
| **1** | **tablespoon minced ginger root** |
| **1** | **tablespoon ground roasted sesame seeds, sunflower seeds, or peanuts** |
| **1** | **teaspoon canola oil** |

Cut the tofu into thin slices, and arrange these between double layers of cotton toweling. Set aside for 15 minutes; then place the pieces at the center of a dry dish towel. Squeeze the tofu firmly to expel as much moisture as possible. Combine the tofu with other ingredients in a large shallow bowl. Mix well; then knead the mixture for about 3 minutes, as if kneading bread. When the dough is smooth and holds together well, moisten your palms with a little oil or warm water, and shape the dough into 8 patties, each 3 to 3 1/2 inches in diameter.

Coat a wok or heavy skillet with canola oil, heat to 300°F, and slide in patties. Cook for 4 to 6 minutes on one side; then turn the patties over and cook for several minutes more or until golden brown. Serve crisp and hot between whole-wheat buns, with burger trimmings. Leftovers may be frozen.

**Exchanges per Serving (patties only):**
Vegetables: 1/8          Legumes: 1          Fats: 1/8

**Nutritional Information per Serving:**
Calories: 125          Protein: 34%          Fiber: 0.5 g
Carbohydrate: 36%          Fat: 30%          Calcium: 125 mg

**Comments:** This is a healthful alternative to hamburgers.

•  •  •  •

# ···· *Tofu Rainbow Sandwich*

*Makes 2 Servings*

| | |
|---|---|
| 10 1/2 | ounces tofu |
| 1 | ounce chopped radish |
| 1 | teaspoon chopped chives |
| 1 | tablespoon chopped parsley |
| | Salt and pepper to taste |
| 4 | endive leaves |
| 2 3/4 | carrots, cut julienne style |
| 4 | tablespoons alfalfa sprouts |
| 4 | slices whole wheat bread |

Place the tofu in a food processor or blender, and blend until creamy. Blend 1/3 of the tofu with paprika and chopped radish, blend 1/3 with chives and parsley, and leave the remaining 1/3 plain. Season with Lite Salt or salt substitute and pepper. Spread each mixture on a slice of bread so that each slice has a different mixture. Stack together and top with the fourth slice. Press together firmly. Slice the stack into 2 portions and garnish with endive, carrots, and alfalfa sprouts.

*Exchanges per Serving:*
Vegetables: 1/2    Grains and starches: 2    Legumes: 1 1/4

*Nutritional Information per Serving:*

| | | |
|---|---|---|
| Calories: 305 | Protein: 25% | Fiber: 3 g |
| Carbohydrate: 48% | Fat: 27% | Calcium: 250 mg |

*Comments:* This sandwich is incredibly easy to make. It is perfect for a quick meal or lunch.

◆ ◆ ◆ ◆

# ····*Tofu Tacos*

*Makes 6 Servings*

| | |
|---|---|
| 12 | ounces tofu |
| 2/3 | cup cooked brown rice or bulgur wheat |
| 1/3 | cup peanuts |
| 1 | green pepper, diced |
| 2 | cloves garlic, crushed |
| 1/4 | teaspoon chili powder |
| 1/3 | cup ketchup |
| 1/2 | teaspoon Lite Salt or salt substitute or 1 tablespoon red miso |
| 1 | tablespoon oil |
| 6 | corn or flour tortillas |
| | Tabasco or taco sauce |
| | Garnishes of your choice, such as chopped tomato, minced onion, and shredded lettuce |

Combine the first 8 ingredients in a large bowl, and mash thoroughly. Heat the oil in a skillet, and fry the tortillas. Fill each tortilla with tofu mixture. Spoon your choice of garnish on the tofu mixture, and season with Tabasco sauce.

*Exchanges per Serving:*

| | |
|---|---|
| Vegetables: 1/6 | Legumes: 1/2 |
| Grains and starches: 1 1/4 | Fats: 1/2 |

*Nutritional Information per Serving:*

| | | |
|---|---|---|
| Calories: 220 | Protein: 21% | Fiber: 2 g |
| Carbohydrate: 49% | Fat: 30% | Calcium: 107 mg |

*Comments:* This is an unusual taco, but it is far more healthful than meat-filled varieties.

◆ ◆ ◆ ◆

# ••••*Tofu and Vegetables over Rice*

*Makes 4 Servings*

| | |
|---|---|
| 1 | tablespoon canola oil |
| 2 | medium onions, cubed |
| 1 | medium green pepper, cubed |
| 1/2 | pound mushrooms, halved |
| 8 | ounces firm tofu, cubed |
| 1/3 | cup sunflower seeds |
| 3/4 | cup water |
| 1/2 | teaspoon basil |
| 1/2 | teaspoon sage |
| 4 | cups cooked brown rice |

In a wok or large skillet, heat the oil; then sauté the onions until limp. Add the green pepper, mushrooms, tofu, sunflower seeds, water, and herbs, and simmer until the vegetables are limp. Serve over cooked brown rice.

*Exchanges per Serving:*
Vegetables: 1/2
Grains and starches: 2
Legumes: 1/2
Fats: 3/4

*Nutritional Information per Serving:*

| | | |
|---|---|---|
| Calories: 310 | Protein: 17% | Fiber: 5 g |
| Carbohydrate: 61% | Fat: 22% | Calcium: 241 mg |

*Comments:* This is a more "American" version of a tofu dish.

◆◆◆◆

# ••••*Vegetarian Chili*

*Makes 8 Servings*

|     |     |
|-----|-----|
| 2   | cups dried kidney beans |
| 1   | tablespoon olive oil |
| 1   | medium onion, peeled and finely chopped |
| 2   | medium cloves garlic, peeled and minced |
| 1   | medium green bell pepper, seeded and finely chopped |
| 1   | medium red bell pepper, seeded and finely chopped |
| 2   | cans (14 1/2 ounces each) low-sodium whole tomatoes, broken apart, with liquid |
| 12  | ounces tomato juice |
| 1   | tablespoon plus 2 teaspoons chili powder |
| 1   | teaspoon dried oregano, crushed |
| 1/2 | teaspoon ground cumin |
| 1/4 | teaspoon cayenne pepper |
| 1/4 | teaspoon Tabasco sauce |
| 1/4 | teaspoon Lite Salt or salt substitute |
| 1 1/2 | cups water |
| 1 1/2 | cups fresh or frozen corn kernels |
| 1   | lime, cut into 8 wedges |

Soak the beans overnight in water until ready to cook; then drain the water off the beans. In a 6-quart pot, add fresh water to cover the beans by 2 inches, and cook the beans for about 1 1/2 hours. Stir in the tomatoes with their liquid, tomato juice, chili powder, oregano, cumin, cayenne, Tabasco, and Lite Salt or salt substitute. Bring just to a boil; then reduce the heat and simmer for 1 hour. Stir often to prevent sticking.

After the beans have cooked for about 40 minutes, prepare the vegetables for cooking. In a wok or pan, heat the olive oil over medium heat. Add the onion, garlic, and green and red bell peppers. Sauté for 5 minutes. Then, 10 minutes before the end of the cooking time, stir this mixture, along with the corn, into the rest of the chili. Serve with lime wedges to squeeze over each serving.

*Exchanges per Serving:*
Vegetables: 1/2
Grains and starches: 1/8
Legumes: 1
Fats: 3/4

*Nutritional Information per Serving:*
Calories: 152
Carbohydrate: 62%
Protein: 18%
Fat: 20%
Fiber: 7 g
Calcium: 66 mg

*Comments:* You'll definitely want another bowl of this super chili.

◆ ◆ ◆

# 10

# ••••Pizza and Pasta

Pizzas and pastas can be extremely healthful foods, especially if prepared with whole-grain flour and without sauces and toppings that are full of cholesterol and saturated fats. The recipes in this chapter accomplish these goals. In fact, the sauces and toppings are actually designed to lower cholesterol levels.

Although many of the recipes call for homemade pasta, if you do not have your own pasta maker, feel free to substitute the appropriate pasta (preferably whole-grain) in the recipe. The sauce recipes can be used with virtually any pasta, and can also serve as the topping for pizza. The pesto recipes are also great as spreads over bread or toast.

Many of the recipes call for soy cheese. Most grocery stores and health-food stores offer various soy cheeses. Mozzarella-flavored varieties will be the best for these recipes. If soy cheese is not available to you, or if you would rather use regular cheeses, choose the so-called "lite" varieties that are lowest in fat.

## ◆ Sauces ◆

# ••••*Marinara Sauce*

*Makes 6 Servings*

| | |
|---|---|
| 2 | tablespoons olive oil |
| 4 | cloves garlic, minced |
| 28 | ounces puréed tomatoes |
| 2 | tablespoons red wine (optional) |
| 1 | teaspoon oregano |
| 1 | teaspoon basil |
| 1/2 | teaspoon thyme |
| 1/4 | teaspoon Lite Salt or salt substitute |
| | Freshly ground pepper to taste |

In a medium-size saucepan, heat the olive oil and garlic, stirring often. Cook until the garlic is golden. Add all the remaining ingredients, and bring to a boil slowly. Simmer for 20 minutes, stirring occasionally.

*Exchanges per Serving:*
Vegetables: 1                    Fats: 1 1/2

*Nutritional Information per Serving:*
Calories: 128            Protein: 5%          Fiber: 1.1 g
Carbohydrates: 34%       Fat: 61%             Calcium: 52 mg

*Comments:* This is the classic Italian-style red sauce. Feel free to add mushrooms, zucchini, and other vegetables to the recipe.

◆◆◆◆

# ••••*Pesto*

*Makes 4 Servings*

|        |                               |
|--------|-------------------------------|
| **2**  | **cups packed fresh basil leaves** |
| **1/3**| **cup olive oil**             |
| **3 or 4** | **cloves garlic**         |
| **1/4**| **cup pine nuts**             |

Wash the basil very well to rid it of any dirt. Combine the ingredients (basil, olive oil, garlic, and pine nuts) in a blender or
food processor, and purée until smooth. Chill until ready to
serve. Bring the pesto to room temperature before serving.

**Exchanges per Serving:**
Vegetables: 1
Fats: 2 3/4

**Nutritional Information per Serving:**
Calories: 168
Carbohydrate: 4%
Protein: 10%
Fat: 86%
Fiber: 1 g
Calcium: 32 mg

**Comments:** Walnuts can substitute for the pine nuts, and 1/2
cup grated Parmesan cheese can be added to the recipe as
well.

◆ ◆ ◆

# ••••*Winter Pesto*

*Makes 6 Servings*

3   cups tightly packed fresh spinach
1   tablespoon dried basil
4   cloves garlic
1/3   cup olive oil
1/3   cup pine nuts
    Dash of Lite Salt or salt substitute

Rinse and dry the spinach. Combine the ingredients in a blender or food processor, and blend until smooth. Refrigerate until ready to use. Bring the pesto to room temperature before serving.

*Exchanges per Serving:*
Vegetables: 1
Fats: 3 1/2

*Nutritional Information per Serving:*
Calories: 174
Carbohydrate: 5%
Protein: 5%
Fat: 90%
Fiber: trace
Calcium: 12 mg

*Comments:* When fresh basil isn't available, this is a great substitute for traditional pesto.

••••

# ···· *Pistachio Pesto*

*Makes 12 Servings (2 tablespoons per serving)*

| | |
|---|---|
| 2 | large garlic cloves |
| 1/2 | teaspoon Lite Salt or salt substitute |
| 1 | 1/2 × 2-inch lemon peel strip, cut into small pieces |
| 2/3 | cup natural roasted pistachio nuts, shelled |
| 1 | cup fresh basil leaves |
| 1/2 | cup fresh parsley leaves |
| 1/2 | cup fresh Italian parsley leaves |
| 1/2 | cup olive oil |
| 1 | tablespoon fresh lemon juice |

Mix the garlic, salt, and lemon peel in a food processor (preferable) or blender to a very fine paste. This should take about 30 seconds. Blend in the pistachios, using several on/off turns until very finely ground. Add the basil and parsley and blend thoroughly, scraping down the sides of bowl frequently. With the machine running, slowly add the olive oil; and mix until creamy. Blend in the lemon juice. Transfer to a jar or other container. Cover with a thin layer of olive oil, and seal tightly. Refrigerate until ready to use (up to 2 weeks later). Bring the pesto to room temperature before serving.

**Exchanges per Serving:**
Vegetables: 1/4                    Fats: 4

**Nutritional Information per Serving:**
Calories: 189          Carbohydrate: 7%          Fiber: 4.3 g
Protein: 2%            Fat: 91%                  Calcium: 132 mg

**Comments:** This pesto is a great change of pace and is delicious spread on bread.

◆ ◆ ◆ ◆

# ••••*Very Red Sauce*

*Makes 4 Servings*

| | |
|---|---|
| 3 | tablespoons olive oil |
| 2 | large red bell peppers or sweet red Italian peppers, seeded and cut into thin strips |
| 1 | large onion, cut into thin strips |
| 1/2 | cup tightly packed, chopped fresh basil leaves or 3 tablespoons dried, crumbled basil |
| 2 | garlic cloves, minced |
| 4 | large ripe tomatoes, cored, seeded, and chopped |
| 1 | 3 × 1/4–inch strip orange peel |
| | Lite Salt or salt substitute |
| | Freshly ground pepper |

Heat the olive oil in a large skillet over medium heat. Add the pepper and onion strips, and cook until the onion is soft and translucent. Stir in the basil and garlic, and cook for 1 minute. Add the tomatoes and orange peel. Increase heat to high and cook, stirring constantly, until the mixture thickens (about 3 minutes). Remove from heat and season with salt and pepper to taste. Transfer to the container and refrigerate. This sauce can be refrigerated for several days or frozen for up to 3 months.

*Exchanges per Serving:*
Vegetables: 1        Fruits: 1/4        Fats: 2 1/4

*Nutritional Information per Serving:*
Calories: 156        Carbohydrate: 12%        Fiber: 2.6 g
Protein: 4%          Fat: 84%                 Calcium: 197 mg

*Comments:* The peppers make this sauce vibrantly red. Feel free to add extra garlic.

♦ ♦ ♦ ♦

# ••••*Tomato Pesto*

*Makes 12 Servings (about 1/4 cup each)*

| | |
|---|---|
| 5 | Italian plum tomatoes |
| 3 | garlic cloves |
| 1 | teaspoon Lite Salt or salt substitute |
| 2/3 | cup toasted blanched almonds |
| 4 | large roasted red peppers, packed in brine, drained |
| 1/8 | teaspoon ground red pepper |
| 1 | cup olive oil |
| 3 | tablespoons red wine vinegar or 2 tablespoons balsamic vinegar |

Char the tomatoes in a broiler or over a flame, turning them until their skins blacken. Peel off the skins. Cut the tomatoes in half, and squeeze to extract seeds and juice. Drain them, cut side down, on paper towels.

Mix the garlic and salt in a food processor (preferable), or finely chop the garlic by hand and add it to a blender along with the salt. If using a food processor, add the almonds and grind finely. Otherwise, finely chop the almonds by hand and add them to the blender. Blend in the peppers using several on/off turns. Add the tomatoes and ground red pepper, and mix until smooth. With the machine running, add the oil in a thin stream. Blend in the vinegar. Transfer to a bowl, cover, and refrigerate for several hours or overnight. Serve at room temperature.

*Exchanges per Serving:*
Vegetables: 1/2          Fats: 4

*Nutritional Information per Serving:*
Calories: 211          Protein: 4%          Fiber: 21 g
Carbohydrate: 4%          Fat: 92%          Calcium: 229 mg

*Comments:* In addition to tasting great over pasta, this pesto is also good as a spread on whole-grain crackers or toast.

••••

## ◆ Pizzas ◆

# ••••*Basic Pizza Dough*

*Makes 4 Servings*

| | |
|---|---|
| 1 | tablespoon fresh yeast or 1/2 tablespoon dried yeast |
| 1/2 | teaspoon raw cane sugar |
| 2/3 | cup warm water |
| 2 | cups plain whole-wheat flour |
| 1 | teaspoon Lite Salt or salt substitute |
| 2 | tablespoons olive oil |

Dissolve the yeast with the sugar in 3 to 4 tablespoons of the warm water. Leave for 5 to 10 minutes in a warm place until activated (it will then appear frothy). Put the flour and salt into a warm bowl; make a well in the center, and pour in the yeast mixture, the warm water, and the olive oil. Mix together until it all comes clean from the sides of the bowl to form a soft, pliable dough, adding a little more warm water if necessary. Turn out onto a floured surface, and knead well for about 5 minutes, until the dough is smooth and fairly elastic. Place the dough in a clean, floured bowl, and cover with a damp cloth. Leave it in a warm place until it doubles in size (from 1 1/2 to 2 hours). Remove the dough from the bowl, and knead it lightly. Roll out or press it into a pizza pan or baking tray. Pat it gently so that it fits, and make the edge of the dough rise a little by tapping it lightly about 1/2 inch from the edge. Add the topping of your choice. Bake in a preheated oven, at 450°F. Make sure that the oven has reached its full heat before you place the pizza in.

*Exchanges per Serving:*
Fruits: 1/8      Grains and starches: 3     Fats: 3/4

*Nutritional Information per Serving:*
Calories: 267          Protein: 9%        Fiber: 6.5 g
Carbohydrate: 73%      Fat: 18%           Calcium: 26 mg

*Comments:* This recipe will make one 12-inch-diameter pizza. Don't be concerned about the 1/2 teaspoon of sugar; it helps the yeast proliferate, and it only contributes 8 calories.

◆◆◆◆

# ◆◆◆◆ *Pizza Margherita*

*Makes 4 Servings*

| | |
|---|---|
| 1 | batch risen Basic Pizza Dough |
| 1 | pound ripe tomatoes, blanched, seeded and chopped |
| | Lite Salt or salt substitute |
| | Freshly ground black pepper |
| 4 | ounces part-skim mozzarella cheese or soy cheese, thinly sliced |
| 4 to 6 | fresh basil leaves or 1 teaspoon dried basil |
| 1/2 | teaspoon oregano |
| 1/2 | teaspoon parsley |
| 4 | tablespoons freshly grated Parmesan cheese |
| 1 | tablespoon olive oil |

Prepare the Basic Pizza Dough recipe. Spread the tomatoes almost to the edge, and season well. Cover with the thinly sliced mozzarella; then top with the basil, parsley, oregano, and Parmesan cheese. Sprinkle a little olive oil over the top, and place in a preheated hot oven (450°F) for 20 minutes, or until the dough has cooked through and the cheese has melted. Serve immediately.

**Exchanges per Serving:**
Vegetables: 1/2   Grains and starches: 3   Meat: 1/2
Fruits: 1/8   Fats: 2 1/2

*Nutritional Information per Serving:*
Calories: 386
Carbohydrate: 51%
Protein: 23%
Fat: 26%
Fiber: 7.25 g
Calcium: 544.5 mg

*Comments:* This is a version of the classic pizza of the Italian region of Liguria, the upper western part of Italy along the Mediterranean Sea.

◆◆◆◆

## ◆◆◆◆ *Pizza with Onions and Olives*

*Makes 4 Servings*

| 1 | batch risen Basic Pizza Dough |
| 2 | large onions |
| 1 | clove garlic |
| 1 | tablespoon olive oil |
| 12 | black olives without pits |
| 2 | tablespoons pine nuts or walnuts |
| 1 | teaspoon dried rosemary |
| | Lite Salt or salt substitute |
| | Freshly ground black pepper |

Shape the dough into individual pizzas, as directed in the Basic Dough Recipe, and set aside. Peel and thinly slice the onions, and separate them into rings. Finely chop the garlic clove. Brush the dough with half of the oil, and cover with the onion rings and garlic. Top with the pitted, halved olives, the pine nuts, and a sprinkling of rosemary. Season with salt and pepper to taste. Spoon the remaining oil over, and bake in a preheated hot oven (450°F) for 20 minutes or until the dough has cooked through. Serve at once.

*Exchanges per Serving:*
Vegetables: 1/2
Grains and starches: 3
Fats: 3 1/2

*Nutritional Information per Serving:*
Calories: 396
Carbohydrate: 55%
Protein: 18%
Fat: 27%
Fiber: 7.7 g
Calcium: 71 mg

*Comments:* Notice that this pizza has no tomato sauce or cheese.

◆◆◆◆

# ••••*Pizza Sicilian Style*

*Makes 4 Servings*

| | |
|---|---|
| 1 | batch risen Basic Pizza Dough |
| 1 1/4 | pounds ripe tomatoes, blanched, seeded, and chopped |
| | Lite Salt or salt substitute |
| | Freshly ground black pepper |
| 4 | cooked fresh or canned artichoke hearts |
| 4 | black olives, without pits |
| 2 | cloves garlic, peeled and sliced |
| 1 | teaspoon oregano |
| 1 | teaspoon crushed red pepper |
| 1 | tablespoon olive oil |
| 1/8 | cup freshly grated Parmesan cheese (optional) |

Prepare the Basic Pizza Dough recipe. Spread the dough in a 9 × 12–inch baking tray. Cover with the tomatoes, almost to the edge, and season well. Slice the artichoke hearts, and put them on top of the tomato. Add the olives, garlic, and oregano. Sprinkle with a little olive oil, and leave to rise in a warm place for 15 minutes. Bake in a preheated hot oven (425°F) for about 30 minutes. Because this pizza has a much thicker base and therefore an increased length of cooking time, it is best to add the cheese at the halfway stage.

*Exchanges per Serving:*
Vegetables: 1    Grains and starches: 3    Fats: 1 1/2

*Nutritional Information per Serving:*
Calories: 357        Protein: 14%        Fiber: 8.25 g
Carbohydrate: 59%    Fat: 27%            Calcium: 194 mg

**Comments:** This pizza offers a nice change from round ones. It makes an excellent party appetizer when sliced into small pieces.

••••

### ◆ Pastas ◆

# ◆◆◆◆ *Basic Processor Pasta*

*Makes 8 Servings*

| 2 1/4 | cups finely sifted whole wheat flour |
| 3 | eggs |
| 1 | teaspoon Lite Salt or salt substitute |

Using a food processor fitted with steel knife, combine all the ingredients, and process until the dough forms a ball. At this point, you may proceed with a pasta machine or by hand.

*Using a pasta machine:* On a well-floured board, divide the dough into 8 equal pieces. Cover with plastic wrap to prevent drying. Set the rollers at their widest setting. Lightly flour the first piece of dough. Run it through the rollers once. Flour it lightly, fold it into thirds, and run it through the rollers again. Repeat the folding and rolling, lightly flouring only when necessary, and pulling the pasta gently to stretch it as it comes out of the machine, until it is as smooth as suede (this may take 6 or more rollings).

Reset the rollers for the next thinner setting. Lightly flour the pasta, but do not fold. Run the pasta through the machine. Repeat on each thinner setting until the dough is as thin as desired. Brush off any excess flour. Repeat the entire process with the remaining dough. Transfer the pasta to a towel, and let it rest until taut but not dry. Cut the pasta on the noodle or vermicelli setting. Separate the strands and let them dry completely on a cloth or a cloth-covered pole.

*By hand:* On a well-floured board, divide the dough into 8 equal pieces. Roll each piece into as thin a rectangle as desired, using as much flour as necessary. Brush off any excess flour with a soft pastry brush. Starting with short end, roll up the dough like a jelly roll. Using a sharp knife, cut the dough into 1/4-inch widths (for noodles) or 1/16-inch widths (for vermicelli). Separate the strands and allow them to dry completely on a cloth or a cloth-covered pole.

*To cook:* Place the pasta in 6 quarts of rapidly boiling water to which 2 tablespoons of Lite Salt or salt substitute have been added. After the water returns to a boil, cook the pasta until al dente (about 30 seconds). Drain well. Homemade pasta can be frozen.

*Exchanges per Serving:*
Grains and starches: 1 1/2
Meat: 1/4

*Nutritional Information per Serving:*
Calories: 142
Protein: 16%
Carbohydrate: 68%
Fat: 16%
Fiber: 3.6 g
Calcium: 24 mg


*Comments:* Many items could be added to this basic recipe. For starters, try adding 1 teaspoon each of dried basil, parsley, and oregano.

◆ ◆ ◆ ◆

# ••••*Angel-hair Pasta with Light Garlic Sauce*

*Makes 4 Servings*

| | |
|---|---|
| 1/2 | pound angel hair pasta |
| 2 | teaspoons olive oil |
| 1 | garlic clove, minced |
| 1/3 | cup minced fresh parsley |
| 1/4 | cup grated soy cheese |
| | Lite Salt or salt substitute to taste |

Bring 2 quarts of water to a boil in a medium-size saucepan. Add the noodles and cook for about 5 minutes. Drain thoroughly. Immediately return the pot to the stove, and add the olive oil and garlic. Cook for 3 minutes over medium heat. Add the drained noodles and parsley, and toss. Add the cheese and salt to taste, and toss again.

*Exchanges per Serving:*
Grains and starches: 1    Legume: 1/4    Fats: 1/2

*Nutritional Information per Serving:*
Calories: 111
Carbohydrate: 63%
Protein: 11%
Fat: 26%
Fiber: 0.5g
Calcium: 25 mg

**Comments:** This is a delicately flavored pasta dish for those not quite accustomed to lots of garlic.

◆ ◆ ◆ ◆

# ••••*Eggplant and Tomatoes over Pasta*

*Makes 8 Servings*

1   large unpeeled eggplant
2   teaspoons Lite Salt or salt substitute
1   tablespoon olive oil
3   medium onions (12 ounces total), quartered and shredded
2   medium garlic cloves, minced
2   large tomatoes (13 ounces total), cored and coarsely chopped
2   cups fresh parsley leaves, minced
2   tablespoons red wine vinegar
1   teaspoon dried oregano, crumbled
    Lite Salt or salt substitute
    Freshly ground pepper
    Basic Processor Pasta, freshly cooked and drained
2   ounces Parmesan cheese, shredded (optional)

Cut the eggplant into "french fries." Or use a food processor fitted with a french-fry disk. Transfer to a colander, sprinkle with Lite Salt or salt substitute, and toss lightly. Weight down with a plate, and let stand for 30 minutes to drain. Pat dry with paper towels.

Heat the oil in a large skillet over medium heat. Add the onion and garlic, and sauté until softened (about 10 minutes). Add the eggplant and cook until tender, shaking the pan constantly to avoid sticking or burning. Add the tomatoes, parsley, vinegar, oregano, salt, and pepper, and heat through, stirring gently with a wooden spoon. Remove from heat.

Toss the pasta with the remaining olive oil. Add the topping and toss again. Taste and adjust the seasoning. Sprinkle with shredded Parmesan, and serve.

*Exchanges per Serving:*
Vegetables: 1/2
Grains and starches: 1 1/2
Fats: 1/2
Meat: 1/4

*Nutritional Information per Serving:*
Calories: 156
Protein: 13%
Carbohydrate: 62%
Fat: 25%
Fiber: 2.6 g
Calcium: 36.7 mg

*Comments:* For a stronger taste, add 1 tablespoon of capers and 12 Italian black olives (leave pits in).

◆◆◆◆

# ••••*Farfalle with Broccoli*

*Makes 4 Servings*

| | |
|---|---|
| 1 | large bunch broccoli (about 1 1/4 pounds) |
| 1 | tablespoon olive oil |
| 3 | large onions, chopped |
| 2 | cloves garlic, minced |
| 1 | pound farfalle (bowtie pasta) |
| 1/4 | teaspoon Lite Salt or salt substitute |
| | Fresh ground pepper |
| 1/2 | cup grated Parmesan cheese |

Bring a large pot of water to boil. Chop the broccoli (about 6 cups). Sauté the onions and garlic over medium heat in a large skillet for 10 minutes. Add the broccoli and cook for about 10 more minutes. Meanwhile, drop the farfalle into the boiling water, and cook it until tender. When the farfalle is cooked, drain and then toss it with the broccoli mixture and cheese. Serve immediately.

*Exchanges per Serving:*
Vegetables: 2
Grains and starches: 1
Fats: 1/2
Meat: 1/2

*Nutritional Information per Serving:*
Calories: 212
Carbohydrates: 53%
Protein: 23%
Fat: 24%
Fiber: 2.5 g
Calcium: 241 mg

*Comments:* Other pasta, such as fettucine, can be substituted, but this recipe works best with farfalle.

◆◆◆◆

# ••••*Linguini with Light Garlic Sauce*

*Makes 4 Servings*

1/2   **pound linguini**
1     **tablespoon olive oil**
1     **clove garlic, minced**
1/3   **cup minced fresh parsley**
1/4   **cup grated soy cheese**
      **Lite Salt or salt substitute to taste**

Bring 2 quarts of water to a boil in a medium-size saucepan. Add the noodles and cook for about 5 minutes. Drain thoroughly. Immediately return the pot to the stove, and add the olive oil and garlic. Cook for 3 minutes over medium heat. Add the drained noodles and parsley, and toss. Add the cheese and salt to taste, and toss again.

*Exchanges per Serving:*
Vegetables: 1/4                    Fats: 3/4
Grains and starches: 1/2          Milk: 1/4

*Nutritional Information per Serving:*
Calories: 87
Carbohydrate: 56%
Protein: 24%
Fat: 20%
Fiber: 0.5g
Calcium: 0.25 mg

*Comments:* Feel free to use more garlic, especially if you have high blood pressure or high cholesterol levels.

••••

# ◆◆◆◆ *Pasta Primavera*

*Makes 4 Servings*

| | |
|---|---|
| 1 | red bell pepper, cut into strips |
| 1 | carrot, peeled and cut into julienne strips |
| 1 | small yellow squash, seeded and cut into strips |
| 4 | ounces snow peas, trimmed and stringed |
| 6 | large tomatoes, chopped |
| 3 | scallions, chopped |
| 4 | ounces fettuccine noodles |
| 1 | teaspoon vegetable oil |
| 1 | tablespoon olive oil |
| 1/2 | cup white wine |
| 4 | tablespoons chopped dill |
| | Lite Salt or salt substitute |
| | Freshly ground black pepper |
| 2 | tablespoons fresh chives |

Bring a medium-size pot of water to a boil. Drop in the bell pepper and carrot. Cook for 30 seconds. Add the squash and snow peas, and cook for 1 minute more. Drain and set aside.

Cook the fettuccine in a large pot of water until tender. Drain and rinse. Set aside.

Heat the olive oil in a medium-size saucepan. Add the tomatoes, wine, salt, pepper, and 2 tablespoons of dill. Cook for 4 to 5 minutes, stirring gently. Toss the fettuccine into the tomato mixture. Add the cooked vegetables, the scallions, the remaining 2 tablespoons of dill and the chives. Toss again and serve immediately.

*Exchanges per Serving:*
Vegetables: 2      Grains and starches: 1/2   Fats: 1

*Nutritional Information per Serving:*

| | | |
|---|---|---|
| Calories: 165 | Protein: 14% | Fiber: 4.8 g |
| Carbohydrate: 58% | Fat: 28% | Calcium: 104 mg |

*Comments:* If you love vegetables with your pasta, this one may quickly become your favorite.

◆◆◆◆

# ••••*Ratatouille over Pasta*

*Makes 6 Servings*

| | |
|---|---|
| 4 | cloves garlic, finely chopped |
| 1 | large onion, chopped |
| 1/8 | cup olive oil |
| 2 | medium green peppers, diced |
| 1 | medium red pepper, diced |
| 1 | medium yellow pepper, diced |
| 2 | medium zucchini, cubed |
| 2 | medium yellow squash, cubed |
| 1 | bunch parsley, chopped |
| 4 | tomatoes, diced |
| 1 | bay leaf |
| 1 | teaspoon basil |
| 1 | teaspoon marjoram |
| 1/4 | teaspoon oregano |
| 1 | teaspoon Lite Salt or salt substitute |
| | Dash pepper |
| 8 | large, firm tomatoes, juiced* |

Sauté the garlic and onion in olive oil. Add the chopped vegetables and seasonings; then add the tomato juice and the pulp from the juicer. Simmer until all the vegetables are tender. Serve over your favorite pasta.

*Exchanges per Serving (without pasta):*
Vegetables: 2                    Fats: 3/4

*Nutritional Information per Serving:*
Calories: 130
Carbohydrate: 55%
Protein: 21%
Fat: 24%
Fiber: 5 g
Calcium: 47 mg

*Comments:* This recipe provides a broad range of nutrients, due to the variety of vegetables it incorporates.

*Tomatoes can be blended, if a juicer is not available.

◆◆◆◆

# ••••*Spaghetti with Garlic and Hot Pepper*

*Makes 6 Servings*

| | |
|---|---|
| 1 | pound whole wheat spaghetti |
| 1 | tablespoon olive oil |
| 1/2 | teaspoon Lite Salt or salt substitute |
| 1 | small red chili pepper or 1/3 teaspoon dried red pepper flakes |
| 2 | tablespoon minced parsley |
| 2 | tablespoons minced fresh garlic |

Bring a large pot of fresh water to a boil. Add the spaghetti and cook at a rolling boil until just tender (al dente). Sauté the garlic, salt, and chili pepper in olive oil for about 3 minutes. Drain the pasta well, place it in a serving bowl, and toss it with the garlic mixture. Add the parsley and toss again.

*Exchanges per Serving:*
Vegetables: 1/6
Grains and starches: 2
Fats: 1/2

*Nutritional Information per Serving:*
Calories: 170
Carbohydrate: 67%
Protein: 13%
Fat: 20%
Fiber: 1.5 g
Calcium: 17 mg

*Comments:* This is extremely quick and easy to prepare—a great meal when you are in a hurry.

◆◆◆◆

# ◆◆◆◆ *Spring Green Pasta*

*Makes 4 Servings*

|   |   |
|---|---|
| 6 | artichoke hearts |
| 6 | thin asparagus spears, cut into 1-inch pieces |
| 8 | ounces pasta |
| 1 | tablespoon olive oil |
| 1/3 | cup chopped scallions |
| 2 | cloves garlic, chopped |
| 12 | black olives |
| 1/2 | cup green peas |
|   | Freshly ground pepper |
|   | Lite Salt or salt substitute |

Bring a large saucepan of water to a boil, and add the asparagus. Simmer for 3 minutes; then drain (keeping the liquid), and set aside.

Bring a large pot of fresh water to a boil. Add the pasta (any pasta will do just fine), and cook at a rolling boil until just tender.

Meanwhile, heat the olive oil in a saucepan. Sauté the scallions and garlic for 3 minutes. Stir in the olives, peas, artichoke hearts, and asparagus, and 1/3 cup of the reserved cooking liquid. Stir well and cook until just heated through (about 2 minutes). Transfer to a serving bowl, and set aside.

Drain the pasta and toss it in the bowl with the sauce until it is well-coated. Season with Lite Salt or salt substitute and pepper to taste. Serve immediately.

*Exchanges per Serving:*
Vegetables: 1 1/2
Grains and starches: 1
Fats: 1

*Nutritional Information per Serving:*
Calories: 193
Carbohydrate: 56%
Protein: 16%
Fat: 28%
Fiber: 2.6 g
Calcium: 63 mg

*Comments:* This extremely healthful pasta dish is super-nutritious.

◆ ◆ ◆

# •••• *Swiss Chard and Garlic with Pasta*

*Makes 4 Servings*

|       |                                                      |
|-------|------------------------------------------------------|
| 1     | pound pasta (linguini, spaghetti, or fettuccine)     |
| 1 1/2 | pounds Swiss chard                                   |
| 1     | tablespoon olive oil                                 |
| 8     | cloves garlic, minced                                |
| 1/4   | teaspoon dried red pepper flakes                     |
| 1/4   | teaspoon Lite Salt or salt substitute                |

Rinse the Swiss chard under cold running water until it is clean. Pat it dry with paper towels. Separate the ribs of the chard from the leaves, and chop each into 1-inch pieces.

Bring a large pot of fresh water to a boil. Add the pasta (any pasta will do just fine), and cook it at a rolling boil until just tender. When the pasta is done, drain it thoroughly; then return it to the pot.

In a large skillet, heat the oil. Add the garlic and red pepper flakes, and cook for 1 minute. Add the chopped Swiss chard ribs, and cook for 2 minutes, stirring often. Add the leaves and cook for 2 minutes more, or until the leaves are slightly wilted.

Place the drained pasta in a serving bowl, and toss on the chard and its sauce. Serve immediately.

**Exchanges per Serving:**
Vegetables: 2      Grains and starches: 1      Fats: 1

**Nutritional Information per Serving:**
Calories: 172          Protein: 12%          Fiber: 3.2 g
Carbohydrates: 58%     Fat: 30%              Calcium: 63 mg

**Comments:** Other greens such as kale or spinach can be used.

•••

# ···· *Vegetable Lasagna*

*Makes 4 Servings*

| | |
|---|---|
| 3 | cups Marinara Sauce |
| 1 | medium zucchini, shredded |
| 6 | uncooked lasagna noodles |
| 4 | cups chopped spinach |
| 3 | cups soy cheese, grated |
| 1 | tablespoon minced fresh or 1 teaspoon dried oregano leaves |

Prepare the Marinara Sauce as specified on page 196; then mix with the zucchini. Spread 1 cup of the mixture in an ungreased rectangular baking dish, 11 × 7 × 1 1/2 inches; top with 3 uncooked noodles. Place the spinach in next, followed by 2 cups of the grated soy cheese, and then the oregano. Spread with 1 cup of the sauce mixture. Top with the remaining noodles, sauce mixture, and soy cheese. Bake uncovered in a 350°F oven until hot and bubbly (about 45 minutes). Let stand for 15 minutes before cutting.

*Exchanges per Serving:*
Vegetables: 2 1/2              Fats: 1 1/2
Grains and starches: 2        Milk: 3/4

*Nutritional Information per Serving:*
Calories: 368        Protein: 14%        Fiber: 2 g
Carbohydrate: 57%    Fat: 29%            Calcium: 448 mg

*Comments:* This recipe can also be topped with sliced mushrooms and/or black olives.

◆◆◆◆

# ••••*Fruits and Desserts*

$E$ating for health does not necessarily mean giving up desserts. If you are trying to lose weight or if you have a blood-sugar disorder like diabetes or hypoglycemia, you will want to use the lower-calorie desserts. If this doesn't apply to you, you should still probably focus on the lower-calorie desserts; but an occassional high-calorie dessert can be a great treat. The important thing in any case is to make sure that the dessert selection fits in with your Healthy Exchange List goals.

## •••• *Apple Crisp with a Twist*

*Makes 8 Servings*

|       |                            |
|-------|----------------------------|
| 6     | green or golden apples     |
| 1     | tablespoon melted butter   |
| 1/3   | teaspoon cinnamon          |
| 2     | tablespoons butter         |
| 1/2   | cup whole wheat flour      |
| 1 1/2 | cups granola               |

Core and slice the apples, leaving their skins on. Place them in an 8-inch-square glass pan, pour butter over the apples, and then sprinkle cinnamon over them. Stir slightly to mix the cinnamon and oil. In a bowl, cut the butter into the flour until the mixture is the size of peas. Fold in the granola, and toss until all is mixed well. Sprinkle over the apple mixture. Bake at 350°F for 40 minutes or until the apples are tender. Cool and serve.

*Exchanges per Serving:*
Fruits: 3/4
Grains and starches: 3/4
Fats: 1 1/4

*Nutritional Information per Serving:*
Calories: 300
Carbohydrate: 58%
Protein: 17%
Fat: 25%
Fiber: 4 g
Calcium: 69 mg

*Comments:* Margarine can be used instead of butter, but butter is better—not only for taste, but also for health reasons.

◆ ◆ ◆

# ••••*Baked Apples*

*Makes 6 Servings*

| | |
|---|---|
| 1/3 | cup golden raisins |
| 2 | tablespoons fresh apple juice |
| 6 | small green cooking apples, cored |
| 1 1/2 | cups fresh apple juice |
| 2 | teaspoons pure vanilla extract |
| 1 | teaspoon cinnamon |
| 1 | teaspoon arrowroot |

Soak the raisins in the apple juice. Remove the peel from the top third of each apple, and arrange the apples in a small baking dish. In a medium-size saucepan, combine the other ingredients and bring to a boil, stirring frequently. Reduce heat, and simmer for 2 to 3 minutes or until slightly thickened. Pour the sauce over the apples. Bake, uncovered, at 350°F for 1 to 1 1/2 hours, basting occasionally, until the apples are easily pierced with a fork. Remove the dish from the oven, and let the apples cool in the sauce. Top each apple with the golden raisins, after discarding the apple juice in which they were soaking. Serve warm.

**Exchanges per Serving:**
Fruits: 1 1/2

**Nutritional Information per Serving:**

| | | |
|---|---|---|
| Calories: 121 | Carbohydrate: 95% | Fiber: 1 g |
| Protein: 1% | Fat: 4% | Calcium: 13 mg |

**Comments:** This is a great dessert to enjoy during the autumn months.

••••

# ••••*Bananas in Berry Sauce*

*Makes 4 Servings*

| | |
|---|---|
| 1 1/2 | cups fresh or frozen unsweetened berries (strawberries, blueberries, boysenberries, raspberries), partially thawed |
| 1/4 | cup fresh apple juice |
| 3 | bananas, halved lengthwise and halved again crosswise |

Purée the berries in a blender. In a nonstick pan or skillet, heat the apple juice; then add the bananas, and sauté for approximately 3 minutes. Pour the puréed berries over the bananas, and heat thoroughly. Serve immediately.

*Exchanges per Serving:*
Fruits: 2

*Nutritional Information per Serving:*
Calories: 170
Carbohydrate: 91%
Protein: 5%
Fat: 4%
Fiber: 3 g
Calcium: 31 mg

*Comments:* This dessert can be made without any cooking as well. Simply delete the apple juice, and pour the puréed berries over the sliced bananas in a dish.

◆◆◆◆

# ••••*Berry Meringue*

*Makes 10 Servings*

| | |
|---|---|
| 3 | cups sliced strawberries |
| 2 | cups cherries, pitted and halved |
| 1/4 | cup frozen apple juice concentrate (unsweetened) |
| 1 | tablespoon fresh lemon juice |
| 1 | tablespoon pectin |
| 1 | teaspoon pure vanilla extract |
| 1 | teaspoon lemon extract |
| 6 | egg whites |

In a medium-size pot, combine all the ingredients except the egg whites. Bring to a boil, stirring constantly. Reduce heat and simmer. Continue stirring constantly for 3 to 5 minutes, until the mixture begins to thicken slightly. Pour it into a bowl to cool briefly. Beat the egg whites until stiff peaks form; then fold into the fruit. Transfer the mixture to a 9 × 13–inch baking dish. Set the dish into a larger oven-proof pan filled with enough boiling water to reach about halfway up the sides of the baking dish. Bake, uncovered, at 375°F for 20 minutes. Remove the baking dish from the water 2 to 3 minutes before the end of the baking period, placing it directly on the oven rack to finish baking. The meringue should brown only slightly. Remove from oven and let sit for 10 minutes or more before serving, or serve chilled.

**Exchanges per Serving:**
Fruits: 1/2          Meat: 1/2

**Nutritional Information per Serving:**

| | | |
|---|---|---|
| Calories: 64 | Carbohydrate: 76% | Fiber: trace |
| Protein: 16% | Fat: 8% | Calcium: 17 mg |

**Comments:** This low-calorie dessert is extremely nutritious.

••••

# ••••*Citrus and Mint*

*Makes 6 Servings*

|     |                                          |
|-----|------------------------------------------|
| 3   | oranges                                  |
| 1   | grapefruit (sweet pink grapefruit is best) |
| 1/2 | cup water                                |
| 1/2 | teaspoon pure vanilla extract            |
| 1/8 | teaspoon ground cloves                   |
| 2   | tablespoons white raisins                |
|     | Fresh mint sprigs (optional)             |

Grate the peels of the oranges and grapefruit into a small saucepan. Be careful to use only the colored part of peels. Peel, seed, and dice the oranges and grapefruit over the saucepan so that no juice is lost. Add the diced fruit, water, vanilla extract, cloves, and raisins to the pan. Bring to a boil; then simmer, uncovered, for 10 minutes. Cool and chill. Spoon into individual serving dishes and garnish with mint sprigs, if desired.

*Exchanges per Serving:*
Fruits: 3/4

*Nutritional Information per Serving:*
Calories: 53
Carbohydrate: 91%
Protein: 7%
Fat: 2%
Fiber: trace
Calcium: 34 mg

*Comments:* This refreshing dessert is good any season of the year.

••••

# ••••*Fruit Combo*

*Makes 8 Servings*

3   medium oranges, peeled and cut up
3   medium pears, cored and cut up
1   cup pitted dark sweet cherries
1   tablespoon fresh lemon juice

Grate 1 teaspoon of peel from the oranges, and set this aside. In a medium-size bowl, combine the oranges, pears, and cherries. Combine the lemon juice and the reserved orange peel. Drizzle over the fruit. Chill.

*Exchanges per Serving:*
Fruits: 1

*Nutritional Information per Serving:*
Calories: 71
Carbohydrate: 90%
Protein: 5%
Fat: 5%
Fiber: 1 g
Calcium: 29 mg

*Comments:* This recipe is rich in vitamin C, flavonoids, and pectin.

◆◆◆◆

# ••••*Melons in a Basket*

*Makes 6 Servings*

3    small cantaloupes
2    cups watermelon balls
2    cups honeydew melon balls
     Fresh mint sprigs

Cut the cantaloupes in half, and scoop out the seeds. Carve balls from the flesh, leaving the cantaloupe shells intact. Combine cantaloupe balls with watermelon and honeydew balls in a medium-size bowl. Toss to blend flavors. Place 1 cup of melon balls in each of the six cantaloupe shells. Garnish with mint sprigs.

*Exchanges per Serving:*
Fruits: 1

*Nutritional Information per Serving:*
Calories: 65
Carbohydrate: 87%
Protein: 7%
Fat: 6%
Fiber: 1 g
Calcium: 16 mg

*Comments:* This is a great dessert to serve during the summer months. It also makes a terrific breakfast.

••••

# ••••*Peach Melba*

*Makes 6 Servings*

3    peaches, peeled, pitted, and halved, or 6 canned peach
     halves (juice pack)
6    tablespoons puréed raspberries
6    tablespoons nonfat vanilla yogurt

Place a peach half in each of six parfait glasses. Top each
peach with 1 tablespoon of raspberry purée, and then with
1 tablespoon of yogurt.

**Exchanges per Serving:**
Fruits: 1/2
Milk: 1/8

**Nutritional Information per Serving:**
Calories: 45
Protein: 6%
Carbohydrate: 92%
Fat: 2%
Fiber: 1 g
Calcium: 5 mg

**Comments:** This very low-calorie dessert is quite satisfying.

◆ ◆ ◆ ◆

# ••••*Pear and Apricot Crisp*

*Makes 6 Servings*

*Fruit Base*

| | |
|---|---|
| 6 | ripe pears |
| 1/2 | cup dried apricots, diced |
| 1 | tablespoon unbleached flour |
| 1/4 | cup honey |

*Topping*

| | |
|---|---|
| 1/2 | cup rolled oats |
| 1/4 | cup whole wheat pastry flour |
| 1/3 | teaspoon cinnamon |
| 1/4 | cup firmly packed light brown sugar |
| 2 | tablespoons butter |
| 1/3 | cup finely chopped walnuts |

Preheat the oven to 400°F, and grease an 8 × 8-inch square pan. Peel and core the pears; then slice them into bite-size pieces, and put them in a medium-size bowl with the apricots. Add the flour and toss to coat; then pour on the honey, and toss again until blended. Transfer this mixture into the baking pan.

Combine the oats, flour, cinnamon, and brown sugar, and mix well. Blend in the butter with the tips of your fingers, until the mixture resembles coarse meal. Stir in the walnuts, and sprinkle the mixture evenly over the pears. Bake for 30 minutes, or until the top is golden. Serve warm or at room temperature.

**Exchanges per Serving:**
Fruits: 2 1/2
Grains and starches: 1
Fats: 1 1/2

*Nutritional Information per Serving:*

| | | |
|---|---|---|
| Calories: 317 | Protein: 6% | Fiber: 5 g |
| Carbohydrates: 67% | Fat: 27% | Calcium: 45 mg |

*Comments:* This is a more filling dessert; watch the calories!

◆◆◆◆

# ◆◆◆◆ *Plantain Patties*

*Makes 2 Servings*

|   |   |
|---|---|
| 2 | ripe plantain bananas |
| 1 | banana |
| 1/8 | teaspoon cinnamon |
| 1/3 | teaspoon sorghum |
| 1/4 | cup water or orange juice |
| 1 | teaspoon butter |

Preheat oven to 350°F. Blend all the ingredients, except the butter, in a blender for 30 seconds at medium speed. Butter a cookie sheet. Using a tablespoon, drop the plantain mixture onto the cookie sheet to form patties. Bake for 7 minutes, or until golden brown; then flip the patties over, and bake for 3 minutes longer. Or heat the butter in a large skillet, over medium-high heat; add teaspoonfuls of the batter, and fry the patties on both sides until golden brown. Serve with jam.

*Exchanges per Serving:*
Fruits: 2 1/2

*Nutritional Information per Serving:*

| | | |
|---|---|---|
| Calories: 212 | Protein: 12% | Fiber: 3 g |
| Carbohydrate: 64% | Fat: 24% | Calcium: 64 mg |

*Comments:* If you have never eaten plantains, give this recipe a try. You'll like it!

◆◆◆◆

# ••••Sautéed Apples and Maple Syrup Topped with Yogurt

*Makes 6 Servings*

| | |
|---|---|
| 6 | medium-size apples, peeled, quartered, and cored |
| 1 | tablespoon butter |
| 5 | tablespoons pure maple syrup |
| 1 1/2 | teaspoon cinnamon |
| 1/4 | teaspoon ground cloves |
| 1 | cup yogurt (nonfat) |
| 2 | tablespoons chopped walnuts |

Cut each apple quarter into 4 slices. Sauté the apples in the butter for 5 minutes. Add 4 tablespoons of the maple syrup, and 1/2 of the cinnamon and cloves. Stir the apples into the mixture to coat. Cook for 7 minutes more, until the apples are tender and the syrup thickens. Scoop the mixture into a medium-size bowl, and chill for 1 hour.

In another medium-size bowl, combine the yogurt, 1 tablespoon of maple syrup, and the remaining cinnamon. Chill for at least 1 hour. When ready to serve, place the apples into each dish. Spoon the yogurt over the top, and garnish with the walnuts.

*Exchanges per Serving:*
Fruits: 2            Fats: 1/2            Milk: 1/6

*Nutritional Information per Serving:*
Calories: 171          Protein: 5%          Fiber: 5.5
Carbohydrate: 72%      Fat: 23%             Calcium: 84

*Comments:* This recipe is also good with pears used in place of apples.

◆ ◆ ◆ ◆

# ••••*Stuffed Peaches with Fresh Cherries and Almonds*

*Makes 4 Servings*

|       |                          |
|-------|--------------------------|
| 1     | cup fresh bing cherries  |
| 1/4   | cup finely chopped almonds |
| 1/3   | teaspoon almond extract  |
| 2     | teaspoons honey          |
| 4     | large ripe peaches       |
|       | Juice of 1/2 lemon       |

Slice each cherry in half, and remove the pit. Slice each half in half again, and mix the pieces in a small bowl with the almonds, almond extract, and honey. Peel the peaches and carefully cut them in half vertically. Remove and discard the stones. If necessary, scoop out a little of the center of each peach half to make it large enough to hold some filling. Put the lemon juice in a small dish, and one at a time toss each peach half in it. This will prevent discoloration. Fill each peach half with an equal portion of the cherry filling, and gently but firmly press it in. Arrange the stuffed peaches in a shallow dish. It is ready to serve.

**Exchanges per Serving:**
Fruits: 1 1/2

**Nutritional Information per Serving:**
| | | |
|---|---|---|
| Calories: 120 | Protein: 7% | Fiber: 3.2 g |
| Carbohydrate: 63% | Fat: 30% | Calcium: 31 mg |

**Comments:** This great-tasting fresh fruit dessert is easy to prepare.

••••

# ••••Tofu-Yogurt

*Makes 1 Serving*

| | |
|---|---|
| 1/2 | block mori-nu tofu |
| 1 to 1 1/2 | cup chopped fresh strawberries, blueberries, or raspberries |
| 1 | teaspoon vanilla extract |
| 1 | teaspoon honey |

Chop up the strawberries in a blender, add the tofu, and blend. Add in the vanilla and honey. The resulting consistency will be similar to that of yogurt.

*Exchanges per Serving:*
Fruits: 2
Legumes: 1 1/2

*Nutritional Information per Serving:*
Calories: 258
Carbohydrate: 48%
Protein: 26%
Fat: 26%
Fiber: 4 g
Calcium: 285 mg

*Comments:* If you suffer from milk allergy or simply desire the nutritional benefits of soy, this is a great alternative to standard yogurt.

◆ ◆ ◆

# •••• *Tropical Parfaits*

*Makes 4 Servings*

1/2   cup vanilla nonfat yogurt
1     medium banana, sliced
      Juice of 1 lime
2     mandarin oranges (or 1 cup pineapple chunks)
      Ground nutmeg to taste

Slip the banana slices into the lime juice to prevent discoloration. In four sherbet dishes, layer the yogurt with a mixture of banana slices, orange sections (or pineapple chunks). Sprinkle each serving with nutmeg. Cover and refrigerate if it is not going to be eaten right away.

*Exchanges per Serving:*
Fruits: 1
Milk: 1/2

*Nutritional Information per Serving:*
Calories: 109
Carbohydrate: 86%
Protein: 9%
Fat: 5%
Fiber: trace
Calcium: 71 mg

*Comments:* Chill the whole fruits for 1 hour before preparing, so that the dish is more refreshing when served.

••••

# •••• *Index*

# More Michael Murray Books for Healthful Living from Prima Publishing

*The Healing Power of Foods*  $16.95

A 448-page companion for *The Healing Power of Foods Cookbook*, this book explains the components of a healthy diet and the health-promoting properties specific foods possess. Sections include: designing a healthy diet, avoiding food allergies, and achieving ideal body weight. Murray also offers specific food prescriptions for common health conditions.

*The Complete Book of Juicing*  $12.95

Dr. Murray combines the latest in scientific research and age-old wisdom with the fabulous health properties in juices to address today's health concerns. From delicious recipes that include complete nutritional analyses to scientifically based health tips, this is the most authoritative juicing book to date! Find out how fresh fruit and vegetable juices can help combat cancer, aging, arthritis, high cholesterol, high blood pressure, kidney stones, ulcers, and dozens of other health conditions.

*The Healing Power of Herbs*  $12.95

The most up-to-date book available on botanical medicines. Covers the remarkable ways in which they work, the very latest scientific findings on their power and efficacy, and the ever-increasing role they are playing in helping people live more healthful lives.

*Encyclopedia of Natural Medicine*  $18.95
co-authored by Joseph Pizzorno, N.D.

Over 600 pages of important information on health maintenance, disease prevention, and treatment. Comprehensively explains the principles of natural medicine and their application in a wide range of chronic illnesses.

# FILL IN AND MAIL . . . TODAY

PRIMA PUBLISHING
P.O. BOX 1260CASP
ROCKLIN, CA 95677

USE YOUR VISA/MC AND ORDER BY PHONE
(916) 786-0449 (M–F 9–4 PST)

I'd like to order the following titles:

| Quantity | Title | Amount |
|---|---|---|
| _____ | _____ | _____ |
| _____ | _____ | _____ |
| _____ | _____ | _____ |
| _____ | _____ | _____ |
| _____ | _____ | _____ |

Subtotal                                      $ _____

Postage & Handling                   $ __3.95__

7.25% Sales Tax
(California only)                             $ _____

TOTAL (U.S. funds only)        $ _____

☐  Check enclosed for $ _____ (payable to Prima Publishing)
Charge my ☐ MasterCard   ☐ Visa

Account No. _____ Exp. Date _____

Signature _____

Your Name _____

Address _____

City/State/Zip _____

Daytime Telephone _____

YOU MUST BE SATISFIED, OR YOUR MONEY BACK!!!
Thank You for Your Order